Modern Critical Interpretations

Samuel Beckett's
Molloy, Malone Dies, The Unnamable

Modern Critical Interpretations

These and other titles in preparation

Samuel Beckett's
Molloy, Malone Dies, The Unnamable

Edited and with an introduction by

Harold Bloom
Sterling Professor of the Humanities
Yale University

Chelsea House Publishers ◇ *1988*
NEW YORK ◇ NEW HAVEN ◇ PHILADELPHIA

© 1988 by Chelsea House Publishers, a division
of Chelsea House Educational Communications, Inc.,
95 Madison Avenue, New York, NY 10016
345 Whitney Avenue, New Haven, CT 06511
5068B West Chester Pike, Edgemont, PA 19028

Introduction © 1988 by Harold Bloom

Printed and bound in the United States of America

10 9 8 7 6 5 4 3 2 1

∞ The paper used in this publication meets the minimum
requirements of the American National Standard for Permanence
of Paper for Printed Library Materials, Z39.48-1984.

Library of Congress Cataloging-in-Publication Data
Samuel Beckett's Molloy, Malone dies, The unnamable.
    (Modern critical interpretations)
    Bibliography: p.
    Includes index.
    Summary: A collection of ten critical essays on three French novels
by Beckett, arranged in chronological order of their original publication.
    1. Beckett, Samuel, 1906–   —Criticism and interpretation.
2. Beckett, Samuel, 1906–   . Innommable. 3. Beckett, Samuel,
1906–   . Molloy. 4. Beckett, Samuel, 1906–   . Malone meurt.
[1. Beckett, Samuel, 1906–   . Malone Dies. 2. Beckett, Samuel,
1906–   . Molloy. 3. Beckett, Samuel, 1906–   . Unnamable.
4. French literature—History and criticism] I. Bloom, Harold. II. Series.
PQ2603.E378Z54   1988   843'.914   87-10087
ISBN 1-55546-057-7 (alk. paper)

Contents

Editor's Note

This book gathers together a representative selection of the best critical interpretations available of Samuel Beckett's trilogy: *Molloy, Malone Dies,* and *The Unnamable*. The critical essays are reprinted in the chronological order of their original publication. I am grateful to Kathryn Ascheim for her aid in editing this volume.

My introduction centers upon the Gnostic element in Beckett's personal vision, which is colored by Schopenhauer's related sense of our catastrophic condition. Georges Bataille, novelist and essayist of the erotic abyss, begins the chronological sequence of criticism with his early account of how *Molloy* gnaws away at existence and the world.

Equally renowned as critic and experimental novelist, Maurice Blanchot finds in the trilogy the timelessness of an endless dying. A very different critic, the Poundian Hugh Kenner gives us a valuable overview of the trilogy, emphasizing its perpetual liveliness even where it works at representing deathliness.

Leo Bersani wittily expresses the struggle of Beckett's fictive characters not to be confused with the voice of their estranged but eloquent author. This struggle is akin to the cancellation of subjectivity by subjectivity, explored by Wolfgang Iser as Beckett's mode of the self endlessly discovering the self, even as a nothingness.

Leslie Hill sees the same problematic process as one in which writing takes the place of the self, a substitution also analyzed by Charlotte Renner, who traces how the trilogy's different narrators merge into one another, and are then usurped by the Unnamable. For Roch C. Smith, this and parallel usurpations combine to make the trilogy into a deliberately failed narrative.

Malone Dies is read as intercalated but certainly not failed narrative by H. Porter Abbott, who recalls us to a sense of Beckett's genre, extreme as Beckett is within that convention. In this book's final essay, Edouard Morot-Sir finds the linguistic lesson of *The Unnamable* to be its discovery of the primitive energy of language in a text that neither begins nor concludes.

Introduction

Jonathan Swift, so much the strongest ironist in the language as to have no rivals, wrote the prose masterpiece of the language in *A Tale of a Tub*. Samuel Beckett, as much the legitimate descendant of Swift as he is of his friend James Joyce, has written the prose masterpieces of the language in this century, sometimes as translations from his own French originals. Such an assertion does not discount the baroque splendors of *Ulysses* and *Finnegans Wake*, but prefers to them the purity of *Murphy* and *Watt*, and of Beckett's renderings into English of *Malone Dies*, *The Unnamable* and *How It Is*. Unlike Swift and Joyce, Beckett is only secondarily an ironist and, despite his brilliance at tragicomedy, is something other than a comic writer. His Cartesian dualism seems to me less fundamental than his profoundly Schopenhauerian vision. Perhaps Swift, had he read and tolerated Schopenhauer, might have turned into Beckett.

A remarkable number of the greatest novelists have found Schopenhauer more than congenial: one thinks of Turgenev, Tolstoy, Zola, Hardy, Conrad, Thomas Mann, even of Proust. As those seven novelists have in common only the activity of writing novels, we may suspect that Schopenhauer's really horrifying system helps a novelist to do his work. This is not to discount the intellectual and spiritual persuasiveness of Schopenhauer. A philosopher who so deeply affected Wagner, Nietzsche, Wittgenstein and (despite his denials) Freud, hardly can be regarded only as a convenient aid to storytellers and storytelling. Nevertheless, Schopenhauer evidently stimulated the arts of fiction; but why? Certain it is that we cannot read *The World as Will and Representation* as a work of fiction. Who could bear it as fiction? Supplementing his book, Schopenhauer characterizes the Will to live:

Here also life presents itself by no means as a gift for enjoyment,

1

but as a task, a drudgery to be performed; and in accordance with this we see, in great and small, universal need, ceaseless cares, constant pressure, endless strife, compulsory activity, with extreme exertion of all the powers of body and mind. . . . All strive, some planning, others acting; the tumult is indescribable. But the ultimate aim of it all, what is it? To sustain ephemeral and tormented individuals through a short span of time in the most fortunate case with endurable want and comparative freedom from pain, which, however, is at once attended with ennui; then the reproduction of this race and its striving. In this evident disproportion between the trouble and the reward, the will to live appears to us from this point of view, if taken objectively, as a fool, or subjectively, as a delusion, seized by which everything living works with the utmost exertion of its strength for something that is of no value. But when we consider it more closely, we shall find here also that it is rather a blind pressure, a tendency entirely without ground or motive.

Hugh Kenner suggests that Beckett reads Descartes as fiction. Beckett's fiction suggests that Beckett reads Schopenhauer as truth. Descartes as a precursor is safely distant; Joyce was much too close, and *Murphy* and even *Watt* are Joycean books. Doubtless, Beckett turned to French in *Molloy* so as to exorcise Joyce, and certainly, from *Malone Dies* on, the prose when translated back into English has ceased to be Joycean. Joyce is to Beckett as Milton was to Wordsworth. *Finnegans Wake*, like *Paradise Lost*, is a triumph demanding study; Beckett's trilogy, like *The Prelude*, internalizes the triumph by way of the compensatory imagination, in which experience and loss become one. Study does little to unriddle Beckett or Wordsworth. The Old Cumberland Beggar, Michael, Margaret of *The Ruined Cottage*; these resist analysis as do Molloy, Malone, and the Unnamable. Place my namesake, the sublime Poldy, in *Murphy* and he might fit, though he would explode the book. Place him in *Watt*? It cannot be done, and Poldy (or even Earwicker) in the trilogy would be like Milton (or Satan) perambulating about in *The Prelude*.

The fashion (largely derived from French misreaders of German thought) of denying a fixed, stable ego is a shibboleth of current criticism. But such a denial is precisely like each literary generation's assertion that it truly writes the common language rather than a poetic diction. Both stances define modernism, and modernism is as old as Hellenistic Alexandria. Callimachus is as modernist as Joyce, and Aristarchus, like Hugh Kenner, is an antiquarian modernist or modernist antiquarian. Schopenhauer dismissed the ego as an illusion, life as torment, and the universe as nothing, and he rightly credited these insights to that great modernist, the Buddha. Beckett too is as modernist as the Buddha, or as Schopenhauer, who disputes with Hume the position of the best writer among philosophers since Plato. I laugh sometimes in reading Schopenhauer, but the laughter is defensive. Beckett provokes laughter, as Falstaff does, or in the mode of Shakespeare's clowns.

II

In his early monograph, *Proust*, Beckett cites Schopenhauer's definition of the artistic procedure as "the contemplation of the world independently of the principle of reason." Such more-than-rational contemplation gives Proust those Ruskinian or Paterian privileged moments that are "epiphanies" in Joyce but which Beckett mordantly calls "fetishes" in Proust. Transcendental bursts of radiance necessarily are no part of Beckett's cosmos, which resembles, if anything at all, the Demiurge's creation in ancient Gnosticism. Basilides or Valentinus, Alexandrian heresiarchs, would have recognized instantly the world of the trilogy and of the major plays: *Waiting for Godot, Endgame, Krapp's Last Tape*. It is the world ruled by the Archons, the *kenoma*, non-place of emptiness. Beckett's enigmatic spirituality quests, though sporadically, for a void that is a fulness, the Abyss or *pleroma* that the Gnostics called both forefather and foremother. Call this a natural rather than a revealed Gnosticism in Beckett's case, but Gnosticism it is nevertheless. Schopenhauer's quietism is at last not Beckett's, which is to say that for Beckett, as for Blake and for the Gnostics, the Creation and the Fall were the same event.

The young Beckett, bitterly reviewing a translation of Rilke into English, memorably rejected Rilke's transcendental self-deceptions, where the poet mistook his own tropes as spiritual evidences:

> Such a turmoil of self-deception and naif discontent gains nothing in dignity from that prime article of the Rilkean faith, which provides for the interchangeability of Rilke and God. . . . He has the fidgets, a disorder which may very well give rise, as it did with Rilke on occasion, to poetry of a high order. But why call the fidgets God, Ego, Orpheus and the rest?

In 1938, the year that *Murphy* was belatedly published, Beckett declared his double impatience with the language of transcendence and with the transcendence of language, while intimating also the imminence of the swerve away from Joyce in the composition of *Watt* (1942–44):

At first it can only be a matter of somehow finding a method by which we can represent this mocking attitude towards the word, through words. In this dissonance between the means and their use it will perhaps become possible to feel a whisper of that final music or that silence that underlies All.

With such a program, in my opinion, the latest work of Joyce has nothing whatever to do. There it seems rather to be a matter of an apotheosis of the word. Unless perhaps Ascension to Heaven and Descent to Hell are somehow one and the same.

As a Gnostic imagination, Beckett's way is Descent, in what cannot be called a hope to liberate the sparks imprisoned in words. Hope is alien to Beckett's mature fiction, so that we can say its images are Gnostic but not its program, since it lacks all program. A Gnosticism without potential transcendence is the most negative of all possible negative stances, and doubtless accounts for the sympathetic reader's sense that every crucial work by Beckett necessarily must be his last. Yet the grand paradox is that lessness never ends in Beckett.

III

"Nothing is got for nothing." That is the later version of Emerson's law of Compensation, in the essay "Power" of *The Conduct of Life*. Nothing is got for nothing even in Beckett, this greatest master of nothing. In the progression from *Murphy* through *Watt* and the trilogy on to *How It Is* and the briefer fictions of recent years, there is loss for the reader as well as gain. The same is true of the movement from *Godot, Endgame* and *Krapp's Last Tape* down to the short plays of Beckett's current and perhaps final phase. A wild humor abandons Beckett, or is transformed into a comedy for which we seem not to be ready. Even an uncommon reader can long for those marvelous Pythagoreans, Wylie and Neary, who are the delight of *Murphy*, or for the sense of the picturesque that makes a last stand in *Molloy*. Though the mode was Joyce's, the music of Wylie and Neary is Beckett's alone:

> "These are dark sayings," said Wylie.
> Neary turned his cup upside down.
> "Needle," he said, "as it is with the love of the body, so with the friendship of the mind, the full is only reached by admittance to the most retired places. Here are the pudenda of my psyche."
> "Cathleen," cried Wylie.
> "But betray me," said Neary, "and you go the way of Hippasos."
> "The Adkousmatic, I presume," said Wylie. "His retribution slips my mind."

"Drowned in a puddle," said Neary, "for having divulged the incommensurability of side and diagonal."

"So perish all babblers," said Wylie. . . .

"Do not quibble," said Neary harshly. "You saved my life. Now palliate it."

"I greatly fear," said Wylie, "that the syndrome known as life is too diffuse to admit of palliation. For every symptom that is eased, another is made worse. The horse leech's daughter is a closed system. Her quantum of wantum cannot vary."

"Very prettily put," said Neary.

One can be forgiven for missing this, even as one surrenders these easier pleasures for the more difficult pleasures of *How It Is*:

> my life above what I did in my life above a little of everything
> tried everything then gave up no worse always a hole a ruin always
> a crust never any good at anything not made for that farrago too
> complicated crawl about in corners and sleep all I wanted I got
> it nothing left but go to heaven

The Sublime mode, according to a great theorist, Angus Fletcher, has "the direct and serious function of destroying the slavery of pleasure." Beckett is certainly the strongest Western author living in the year 1987, the last survivor of the sequence that includes Proust, Kafka and Joyce. It seems odd to name Beckett, most astonishing of minimalists, as a representative of the Sublime mode, but the isolation and terror of the High Sublime return in the catastrophe creations of Beckett, in that vision Fletcher calls "catastrophe as a gradual grinding down and slowing to a dead stop." A Sublime that moves towards silence necessarily relies upon a rhetoric of waning lyricism, in which the entire scale of effects is transformed, as John Hollander notes:

> Sentences, phrases, images even, are the veritable arias in the plays
> and the later fiction. The magnificent rising of the kite at the end
> of *Murphy* occurs in a guarded but positive surge of ceremonial
> song, to which he will never return.

Kafka's Hunter Gracchus, who had been glad to live and was glad to die, tells us that "I slipped into my winding sheet like a girl into her marriage dress. I lay and waited. Then came the mishap." The mishap, a moment's error on the part of the death-ship's pilot, moves Gracchus from the heroic world of romance to the world of Kafka and of Beckett, where one is neither alive nor dead. It is Beckett's peculiar triumph that he disputes with Kafka the dark eminence of being the Dante of that world. Only Kafka, or Beckett, could have written the sentence in which Gracchus sums up the dreadfulness of his condition: "The thought of helping me is an illness that has to be cured by taking to one's bed." Murphy might have said that; Malone is beyond saying anything so merely expressionistic. The "beyond" is where Beckett's later fictions and plays reside. Call it the silence, or the abyss, or the reality beyond the pleasure principle, or the metaphysical or spiritual reality of our existence at last exposed, beyond further illusion. Beckett cannot or will not name it, but he has worked through to the art of representing it more persuasively than anyone else.

IV

"Dante and the Lobster," written in 1932, is the first story in Beckett's collection, *More Pricks Than Kicks* (1934). Its first paragraph is a true starting-point for Beckett's achievement in prose fiction, of which the crown is the trilogy: *Molloy, Malone Meurt,* and *L'Innommable*, all written from 1946 to 1950, and published 1951–53. Belacqua's epiphany, in his story's initial paragraph, is achieved as much against Dante as through him:

> It was morning and Belacqua was stuck in the first of the canti in the moon. He was so bogged that he could move neither backward nor forward. Blissful Beatrice was there, Dante also, and she explained the spots on the moon to him. She shewed him in the first place where he was at fault, then she put up her own explanation. She had it from God, therefore he could rely on its being accurate in every particular. All he had to do was to follow her step by step. Part one, the refutation, was plain sailing. She made her point clearly, she said what she had to say without fuss or loss of time. But part two, the demonstration, was so dense that Belacqua could not make head or tail of it. The disproof, the reproof, that was patent. But then came the proof, a rapid shorthand of the real facts, and Belacqua was bogged indeed. Bored also, impatient to get on to Piccarda. Still he pored over the enigma, he would not concede himself conquered, he would understand at least the meanings of the words, the order in which they were spoken and the nature of the satisfaction that they conferred on the misinformed poet, so that when they were ended he was refreshed and could raise his heavy head, intending to return thanks and make formal retraction of his old opinion.

Belacqua, in Dante, is a long way from Beatrice, being one of the indolent who rest in the shade of a great boulder, in Canto IV of the *Purgatorio*. In Beckett's favorite posture, Belacqua "sat clasping his knees and holding his face low down between them." Dante, recognizing an old acquaintance, is charmed into a smile and asks Belacqua why he remains seated. The reply is Beckett's credo, or a central part of it.

> O brother, why go up, since God's angel who sits in the gateway would not let me pass on to the sufferings? First the heavens must wheel about me, while I wait outside, as long as they did in my lifetime, because until the very end I postponed any good sighs. Unless I am aided first by prayer rising from a heart living in grace, since other prayers are not heard in Heaven.

Belacqua is Beckett, but not yet a Gnostic Beckett, who is to come as Molloy, Malone, and the Unnamable. Eventually Belacqua will get up the mountain, whereas Molloy and the others will not, since they know nothing of Purgatory. Beckett's trilogy, like *Waiting for Godot*, takes place in the *kenoma*, an emptied-out cosmos, where Molloy survives by means of his sucking-stones:

> But don't imagine my region ended at the coast, that would be a grave mistake. For it was this sea too, its reefs and distant islands, and its hidden depths. And I too once went forth on it, in a sort of oarless skiff, but I paddled with an old bit of driftwood. And I sometimes wonder if I ever came back, from that voyage. For if I see myself putting to sea, and the long hours without landfall, I do not see the return, the tossing on the breakers, and I do not hear the frail keel grating on the shore. I took advantage of being at the seaside to lay in a store of sucking-stones. They were pebbles but I call them stones. Yes, on this occasion I laid in a considerable store. I distributed them equally among my four pockets, and sucked them turn and turn about. This raised a problem which I first solved in the following way. I had say sixteen stones, four in each of my four pockets these being the two pockets of my trousers and the two pockets of my greatcoat. Taking a stone from the right pocket of my greatcoat, and putting it in my mouth, I replaced it in the right pocket of my greatcoat by a stone from the right pocket of my trousers, which I replaced by a stone from the left pocket of my trousers, which I replaced by a stone from the left pocket of my greatcoat, which I re-

placed by the stone which was in my mouth, as soon as I had finished sucking it. Thus there were still four stones in each of my four
pockets, but not quite the same stones. And when the desire to
suck took hold of me again, I drew again on the right pocket
of my greatcoat, certain of not taking the same stone as the last
time. And while I sucked it I rearranged the other stones in the
way I have just described. And so on. But this solution did not
satisfy me fully. For it did not escape me that, by an extraordinary hazard, the four stones circulating thus might always be
the same four. In which case, far from sucking the sixteen stones
turn and turn about, I was really only sucking four, always the
same, turn and turn about. But I shuffled them well in my pockets,
before I began to suck, and again, while I sucked, before transferring them, in the hope of obtaining a more general circulation
of the stones from pocket to pocket. But this was only a makeshift
that could not long content a man like me. So I began to look
for something else. And the first thing I hit upon was that I might
do better to transfer the stones four by four, instead of one by
one, that is to say, during the sucking, to take the three stones
remaining in the right pocket of my greatcoat and replace them
by the four in the right pocket of my trousers, and these by the
four in the left pocket of my trousers, and these by the four in
the left pocket of my greatcoat, and finally these by the three from
the right pocket of my greatcoat, plus the one, as soon as I had
finished sucking it, which was in my mouth. Yes, it seemed to
me at first that by so doing I would arrive at a better result. But
on further reflection I had to change my mind and confess that
the circulation of the stones four by four came to exactly the same
thing as their circulation one by one. For if I was certain of finding each time, in the right pocket of my greatcoat, four stones
totally different from their immediate predecessors, the possibility nevertheless remained of my always chancing on the same stone,
within each group of four, and consequently of my sucking, not
the sixteen turn and turn about as I wished, but in fact four only,
always the same, turn and turn about. So I had to seek elsewhere
than in the mode of circulation. For no matter how I caused the
stones to circulate, I always ran the same risk. It was obvious
that by increasing the number of my pockets I was bound to increase my chances of enjoying my stones in the way I planned,
that is to say one after the other until their number was exhausted.
Had I had eight pockets, for example, instead of the four I did

have, then even the most diabolical hazard could not have prevented
me from sucking at least eight of my sixteen stones, turn and
turn about. The truth is I should have needed sixteen pockets
in order to be quite easy in my mind.

These stones presumably could not be turned into bread by Christ, since
the Gnostic Christ never became flesh, and so dwelt among us only as a phantom. But that is how all of us dwell upon earth in the trilogy; there has
been a *kenosis* of the ego, and the sucking-stones afford all the communion
we could hope to sustain. The word "trim" sings within us like a verse of
the prophets because the principle of trimming gets us beyond the impossible necessity of having sixteen pockets. Like Molloy, we can divide our sucking-
stones into four groups of four each, or follow any other private ritual as
Gnostic trimmers. What we cannot do is represent either ourselves or anyone
else, no matter how negative the representation. Molloy, like Murphy, is
still a version of Beckett, however attenuated, yet this is not a version of
a consciousness, but only of a writer obsessed with the blind activity of writing.
And since Moran, the quester for Molloy, in some sense writes him, we are
confronted by an art that forgoes mimesis not for an antimimesis, but for
a super-mimesis, in which every figure is written by another figure who is
written by another endlessly in a vertigo of Gnostic (rather than Heideg-
gerian) *thrown-ness*. All references, as Wolfgang Iser remarked, are exposed
as pragmatic fictions.

Hugh Kenner, subtly baptizing Beckett's imagination, reads the trilogy
as an implicit judgment upon the Cartesian dehumanization of man. Beckett
seems to me far more archaic than that, as archaic as Schopenhauer. The protagonists of the trilogy are not ghosts inhabiting machines, but sparks of
light uneasily flickering inside ghosts. Dehumanization, as part of Beckett's
given, has nothing to do with the Enlightenment, and everything to do with
a far more aboriginal catastrophe, a creation-fall brought about by a blunder-
ing Demiurge. Molloy's sucking-stones are the Gnostic version of the great
Western literary trope or fiction of the leaves, perhaps by an association of
stones to loaves to leaves, since Malone has pockets full of pebbles that "stand
for men and their seasons." You can write an "Ode to the West Wind"
or a lyric meditation like Stevens's "The Course of a Particular" in an extension of the fiction of the leaves, but what can you do with the trope of the
sucking-stones? Virgil's dead souls, fluttering like leaves, stretch forth their
hands out of love for the farther shore. Stones do not stretch, and few passages
in modern literature frighten me as much as the conclusion of *Malone Dies*,
where I would prefer Charon as boatman to Beckett's uncanny Lemuel:

Finally she moved away again, followed by Ernest carrying the hamper in his arms. When she had disappeared Lemuel released Macmann, went up behind Maurice who was sitting on a stone filling his pipe and killed him with the hatchet. We're getting on, getting on. The youth and the giant took no notice. The thin one broke his umbrella against the rock, a curious gesture. The Saxon cried, bending forward and slapping his thighs, Nice work, sir, nice work! A little later Ernest came back to fetch them. Going to meet him Lemuel killed him in his turn, in the same way as the other. It merely took a little longer. Two decent, quiet, harmless men, brothers-in-law into the bargain, there are billions of such brutes. Macmann's huge head. He has put his hat on again. The voice of Lady Pedal, calling. She appeared, joyous. Come along, she cried, all of you, before the tea gets cold. But at the sight of the late sailors she fainted, which caused her to fall. Smash her! screamed the Saxon. She had raised her veil and was holding in her hand a tiny sandwich. She must have broken something in her fall, her hip perhaps, old ladies often break their hips, for no sooner had she recovered her senses than she began to moan and groan, as if she were the only being on the face of the earth deserving of pity. When the sun had vanished, behind the hills, and the lights of the land began to glitter, Lemuel made Macmann and the two others get into the boat and got into it himself. Then they set out, all six, from the shore.

Gurgles of outflow.

This tangle of grey bodies is they. Silent, dim, perhaps clinging to one another, their heads buried in their cloaks, they lie together in a heap, in the night. They are far out in the bay. Lemuel has shipped his oars, the oars trail in the water. The night is strewn with absurd

absurd lights, the stars, the beacons, the buoys, the lights of earth and in the hills the faint fires of the blazing gorse. Macmann, my last, my possessions, I remember, he is there too, perhaps he sleeps. Lemuel

Lemuel is in charge, he raises his hatchet on which the blood will never dry, but not to hit anyone, he will not hit anyone, he will not hit anyone any more, he will not touch anyone any more, either with it or with it or with it or with or or with it or with his hammer or with his stick or with his flat or in thought in dream I mean never he will never

or with his pencil or with his stick or

or light light I mean

never there he will never

never anything

there

any more

Lemuel, like all the violent in Beckett, is what the Gnostics called an Archon, one of the rulers of the darkness of this life. The Unnamable is the final dissenter in the *kenoma* of the Archons, changing all that is left of the spark's desire to go on illuminating a darkness as much the soul's as the body's:

or it's the murmurs, the murmurs are coming, I know that well, no, not even that, you talk of murmurs, distant cries, as long as you can talk, you talk of them before and you talk of them after, more lies, it will be the silence, the one that doesn't last, spent listening, spent waiting, for it to be broken, for the voice to break it, perhaps there's no other, I don't know, it's not worth having, that's all I know, it's not I, that's all I know, it's not mine, it's the only one I ever had, that's a lie, I must have had the other, the one that lasts, but it didn't last, I don't understand, that is to say it did, it still lasts, I'm still in it, I left myself behind in it, I'm waiting for me there, no, there you don't wait, you don't listen, I don't know, perhaps it's a dream, all a dream, that would surprise me, I'll wake, in the silence, and never sleep again, it will be I, or dream, dream again, dream of a silence, a dream silence, full of murmurs, I don't know, that's all words, never wake, all words, there's nothing else, you must go on, that's all I know, they're going to stop, I know that well, I can feel it, they're going to abandon me, it will be the silence, for a moment, a good few moments, or it will be mine, the lasting one, that didn't last, that still lasts, it will be I, you must go on, I can't go on, you must go on, I'll go on, you must say words, as long as there are any, until they find me, until they say me, strange pain, strange sin, you must go on, perhaps it's done already, perhaps they have said me already, perhaps they have carried me to the threshold of my story, before the door that opens on my story, that would surprise me, if it opens, it will be I, it will be the silence, where I am, I don't know, I'll never know, in the silence you don't know, you must go on, I can't go on, I'll go on.

Molloy's Silence

Georges Bataille

What the author of *Molloy* has to tell us is, if you please, the most unabashedly unbearable story in the world: nothing in it but an exorbitant imagination; the whole thing is fantastic, extravagant, sordid to be sure, but of a wonderful sordidness; to be more precise, *Molloy* is a sordid wonder. No other story could be so necessary and so convincing at the same time; what *Molloy* reveals is not simply reality but reality in its pure state: the most meagre and inevitable of realities, that fundamental reality continually soliciting us but from which a certain terror always pulls us back, the reality we refuse to face and into which we must ceaselessly struggle not to sink, known to us only in the elusive form of anguish.

If I were indifferent to cold, hunger, and the myriad difficulties that overwhelm a man when he abandons himself to nature, rain, and the earth, to the immense quicksand of the world and of things, I myself would be the character Molloy. I can say something more about him, and that is that both you and I have met him: seized by a terrified longing, we have encountered him on street corners, an anonymous figure composed of the inevitable beauty of rags, a vacant and indifferent expression, and an ancient accumulation of filth; he was *being, defenseless* at last, an enterprise, as we all are, that had ended in shipwreck.

There is in this reality, the essence or residue of being, something so *universal*, these complete *vagabonds* we occasionally encounter but immediately *lose* have something so essentially indistinct about them, that we cannot imagine anything more anonymous. So much so that this name *vagabond* I have just written down misrepresents them. But that of *wretch*, which has perhaps

From *Samuel Beckett: The Critical Heritage*, edited by Lawrence Graves and Raymond Federman. © 1979 by Lawrence Graves and Raymond Federman. Routledge & Kegan Paul, 1979.

the advantage over the other of an even greater indeterminacy, is equally a misrepresentation. What we have here is so assuredly the essence of being (but this expression alone, "essence of being," could not determine the *thing*) that we need not hesitate: to *this*, we cannot give a name, it is indistinct, necessary, and elusive, quite simply, it is *silence*. This thing we name through sheer impotence *vagabond* or *wretch*, which is actually *unnamable* (but then we find ourselves entangled in another word, *unnamable*), is no less mute than death. Thus we know in advance that the attempt to speak to this phantom haunting the streets in broad daylight is futile. Even if we knew something about the precise circumstances and conditions of his life (?) and his wretchedness, we would have made no headway: this man, or rather this being whose speech, sustaining him, might have made him human — whatever speech subsists or rather exhausts itself in him no longer sustains him, and similarly, speech no longer reaches him. Any conversation we might have with him would be only a phantom, an appearance of conversation. It would delude us, referring us to some appearance of humanity, to something other than this *absence* of humanity heralded by the derelict dragging himself through the streets, who fascinates us. I recall having had at an early age a long conversation with a *vagabond*. It lasted the better part of a night I spent waiting for a train in a small station. He, of course, was not waiting for any train; he had simply taken shelter in the waiting-room, and he left me towards morning to go to make some coffee over a campfire. He was not precisely the sort of being I am speaking of; he was even talkative, more so than I was, perhaps. He seemed satisfied with his life, and being an old man, amused himself by expressing his happiness to the adolescent I was, listening to him with admiration. Yet the memory he left with me, and the amazed terror it still arouses in me, continue to remind me of the silence of animals. (This encounter impressed me so deeply that soon afterwards I began to write a novel in which a man who has met him in the countryside kills him, perhaps in hopes of gaining access to the animality of his victim.) On another occasion, while driving with friends, we found in broad daylight, in a forest, a man alongside the road stretched out on the grass and, so to speak, in the water, in a pouring rain. He was not asleep, perhaps he was ill; he did not respond to our questions. We offered to drive him to a hospital: I seem to recall that he still did not answer, or that if he bothered to respond, it was with a vague grunt of refusal.

We should make this essential point clear: there is no reason to think that Samuel Beckett meant to describe this "essence of being" or this "absence of humanity" I have been speaking of. It even seems to me unlikely that he intended Molloy to be a typical vagabond (or whatever unnamable thing this name indicates), in the same way that Molière intended Harpagon to be a typical miser, Alceste a typical misanthrope. To tell the truth, we hardly know anything about the intentions of Molloy's creator, and on the whole, what we do know about him amounts to nothing. Born in 1906, Irish, he was a friend of Joyce, and has even remained his disciple to some extent. His friendships—or his relations—place him, it seems, in the milieu Joyce was familiar with in France. Before the war he wrote a novel in English, but at the same time published his own French translation, and being bilingual, he seems to have a decided preference for French. The obvious influence of Joyce on Beckett, however, is far from being the key to the latter. At most the two writers show a similar interest in the chaotic possibilities given in the free—nevertheless controlled and composed, yet violent—play of language. And certainly this sort of confidence, with one eye open perhaps but apparently unseeing, in the creative violence of language locates precisely the abyss that separates Beckett from Molière. But after all, would not this abyss be similar to the one that separates the misanthrope or the miser from the *absence* of humanity and the *amorphous* personality of Molloy? Only an unrestrained flow of language would have the power to achieve this absence (this lack of restraint, this flow would themselves be equivalent to a negation, to the absence of that "discourse" that gives to the figures of miser and misanthrope the completed *form* without which we would be unable to imagine them). And conversely, it may be that the freedom of a writer who no longer reduces writing to a means of expressing his meaning, who consents to respond to possibilities present, though chaotically mingled, in those deep currents that flow through the oceanic agitation of words, results of its own accord, yielding to the weight of destiny, in the *amorphous* figure of *absence*.

"All I know," says Molloy (or the author), "is what the words know, and the dead things, and that makes a handsome little sum, with a beginning, a middle and an end as in the well-built phrase and the long sonata of the dead. And truly it little matters what I say, this or that or any other thing. Saying is inventing. Wrong, very rightly wrong. You invent nothing, you think you are inventing, you think you are escaping, and all you do is stammer out your lesson, the remnants of a pensum one day got by heart and long forgotten, life without tears, as it is wept." This is not a school's manifesto, not a manifesto at all but one expression, among others, of movements that go beyond any school and that want literature, finally, to make language into a facade, eroded by the wind and full of holes, that would possess the authority of ruins.

Thus, without, or because of, and even for lack of having intended to do so, literature as inevitably as death—compelled by the imperative necessity characteristic of every road that leads to a summit and that no longer allows any room for choice—leads to the fathomless misery of *Molloy*. This irresistible movement seems to follow the most arbitrary of whims, yet it is governed by the weight of fatality. Language is what determines this regulated world, whose significations provide the foundation for our cultures, our activities and our relations, but it does so in so far as it is reduced to a means of these cultures, activities and relations; freed from these servitudes, it is nothing more than a deserted castle whose gaping cracks let in the wind and rain: it is no longer the signifying word, but the defenseless expression death wears as a disguise.

A disguise nevertheless. Death itself would be that final silence that has never been attenuated by its imitations. Literature, on the other hand, lines up a torrent of incongruous words next to silence. Though it allegedly conveys the same meaning as death, this silence is only a parody of the latter. Nor is it, moreover, genuine language: it is even possible that *literature* may have the same fundamental meaning as silence, but it recoils before the final step that silence would be. Likewise this Molloy, who is its incarnation, is not precisely a dead man. The profound apathy of death, its indifference to every possible thing, is apparent in him, but this apathy would encounter in death itself its own limit. The interminable meandering in the forest of this death's equivalent on crutches is, nevertheless, different from death in one respect: that out of habit, or for the sake of persevering more diligently in death and in the amorphous negation of life—in the same way that literature is in the end silence in its negation of meaningful language, but remains what it is, literature—the *death* of Molloy is *in* this death-obsessed life, in which not even the desire to forsake it is permitted.

"But did it make such a difference after all, as far as the pain was concerned," says Molloy (disturbed though not distressed by an aggravation of his infirmities), "whether my leg was free to rest or whether it had to work? I think not. For the suffering of the leg at rest was constant and monotonous. Whereas the leg condemned to the increase of pain inflicted by work knew the decrease of pain dispensed by work suspended, the space of an instant. But I am human, I fancy, and my progress suffered, from this state of affairs, and from the slow and painful progress it had always been, whatever may have been said to the contrary, was changed, saving your presence, to a veritable calvary, with no limit to its stations and no hope of crucifixion, though I say it myself, and no Simon, and reduced me to frequent halts. Yes, my progress reduced me to stopping more and more often, it was the only way to progress, to stop. And though it is no part of my tottering intentions to treat here in full, as they deserve, these brief moments of the immemorial expiation, I shall nevertheless deal with them briefly, out of the goodness of my heart, so that my story, so clear till now, may not end in darkness, the darkness of these towering forests, these giant fronds, where I hobble, listen, fall, rise, listen and hobble on, wondering sometimes, need I say, if I shall ever see again the hated light, at least unloved, stretched palely between the last boles, and my mother, to settle with her, and if I would not do better, at least just as well, to hang myself from a bough, with a liane. For frankly light meant nothing to me now, and my mother could scarcely be waiting for me still, after so long. And my leg, my legs. But the thought of suicide had little hold on me, I don't know why, I thought I did, but I see I don't."

It goes without saying that so faithful an attachment to life can only be unreasonable; indeed it is pointless to mention that the object of this fidelity is really death: this would only mean something if death—or existence in death—or death in existence—meant anything; now the only meaning in all this lies in the fact that nonsense in its own way makes sense, a parody of meaning, perhaps, but finally a distinct meaning, which is to obscure within us the world of significations. Such in fact is the blind purpose of this brisk narrative, borne at length by such an unquenchable verve that we read it with no less impatient interest than a thrilling adventure novel.

> Lasciate ogni speranza voi qu'entrate. (Abandon all hope, ye that enter.)

Such could well be the epigraph for this absolutely striking book, whose exclamation, uninterrupted by paragraphs, explores with unflinching irony the extreme possibilities of indifference and misery. An isolated passage gives only a lifeless, feeble, impression of this vast journey, which the narrative paradoxically arranges into an immense, shattering epic, borne along in an irresistible, inhuman onrush (as a matter of fact it is difficult to take Molloy at his word when he chances to call himself human, for in the depths of misery, he monstrously allows himself the incongruity, obscenity and moral indifference that all of *humanity*, anxious and afflicted with scruples, would deny themselves). *Abandon all hope.* . . . frankly speaking, is accurate only in one sense, and the violence of irony imposes itself almost as soon as these funereal words are pronounced. For at the very moment when he is limping along, brutalized by the police, molested, Molloy notes its precise limit: "While still putting my best foot foremost," he says in his naïveté, "I gave myself up to that golden moment, as if I had been someone else. It was the hour of rest, the forenoon's toil ended, the afternoon's to come. The wisest perhaps, lying in the squares or sitting on their doorsteps, were savouring its languid ending, forgetful of recent cares, indifferent to those at hand. . . . Was there one among them to put himself in my place, to feel how removed I was then from him I seemed to be, and in that remove what strain, as of hawsers about to snap? It's possible. Yes, I was straining towards those spurious deeps, their lying promise of gravity and peace, from all of my old poisons I struggled towards them, safely bound. Under the blue sky, under the watchful gaze. Forgetful of my mother, set free from the act, merged in this alien hour, saying, Respite, respite." Strictly speaking it would have been more effective to let this aspect remain implicit: I do not mean to say that the book would have definitely gained by this, but there are one or two brilliant phrases here that are out of tune. The reader's own subtlety of perception could have come to his assistance: that subtlety would have responded to the failure inherent in all of literature, which only with difficulty and in a burst of brutal naïveté overcomes the movement that draws it towards confusion. In part this passage is flawed, out of place, but it provides us with the key to the narrative, in which the tension that rivets us to depression never lets up. Certainly, here all reasonable *hopes* and plans are engulfed in indifference. But perhaps it is to be assumed that, in the moment given here, within the limits of this present time, there is nothing that matters, nothing that could matter. Nothing, not even a persistent feeling of inferiority, not even a destiny linking the hero to an expiation of his sins, which could in no way abase or humiliate him: it pursues its course doggedly, without anxiety, in an obstinate silence: "But perhaps I was mistaken, perhaps I would have been better advised to stay in the forest, perhaps I could have stayed there, without remorse, without the painful impression of committing a fault, almost a sin. For I have greatly sinned, at all times, greatly sinned against my prompters. And if I cannot decently be proud of this I see no reason either to be sorry. But imperatives are a little different, and I have always been inclined to submit to them, I don't know why. For they never led me anywhere, but tore me from places where, if all was not well, all was no worse than anywhere else, and then went silent, leaving me stranded. So I knew my imperatives well, and yet I submitted to them. It had become a habit. It is true they nearly all bore on the same question, that of my relations with my mother, and on the importance of bringing as soon as possible some light to bear on these and even on the kind of light that should be brought to bear and the most effective means of doing so. Yes, these imperatives were quite explicit and even detailed until, having set me in motion at last, they began to falter, then went silent, leaving me there like a fool who neither knows where he is going nor why he is going there." In the end this expiation, to which Molloy is submissive, requires him to leave the forest as quickly as possible. Although it eludes him every time he becomes aware of it, it imposes itself upon him with such convincing force that in his bewilderment there is nothing he will not do to obey it. No longer able to walk, he continues his journey crawling like a slug: "Flat on my belly, using my crutches like grapnels, I plunged them ahead of me into the undergrowth, and when I felt they had a hold, I pulled myself forward, with an effort of the wrists. For my wrists were still quite strong, fortunately, in spite of my decrepitude, though all swollen and racked by a kind of chronic arthritis probably. That then briefly is how I went about it. The advantage of this mode of locomotion compared to others, I mean those I have tried, is this, that when you want to rest you stop and rest, without further ado. For standing there is no rest, nor sitting either. And there are men who move about sitting, and even kneeling, hauling themselves to right and left, forward and backward, with the help of hooks. But he who moves in this way, crawling on his belly, like a reptile, no sooner comes to rest than he begins to rest, and even the very movement is a kind of rest, compared to other movements, I mean those that have worn me out. And in this way I moved onward in the forest, slowly, but with a certain regularity, and I covered my fifteen paces, day in, day out, without killing myself. And I even crawled on my back, plunging my crutches blindly behind me into the thickets, and with the black boughs for sky to my closing eyes. I was on my way to mother. And from time to time I said, Mother, to encourage me I suppose. I kept losing my hat, the lace had broken long ago, until in a fit of temper I banged it down on my skull with such violence that I couldn't get it off again. And if I had met any lady friends, if I had had any lady friends, I would have been powerless to salute them correctly."

But, you may say, this sordid extravagance is of little importance, these immense phantasmagorias bore us, they leave us strictly cold. This is possible. But there is a primary reason why this absence of interest is not necessarily justifiable: the power and passion of the author force us to become brutally convinced of the contrary. This frantic progress toward ruin that animates the book, which, being the author's attack on the reader, is such that not for an instant is the latter given the leisure to withdraw into indifference — could it have been produced if so persuasive a conviction did not originate in some powerful motive?

As I have said, we have no right to assume that the author began with a detailed plan in mind. Doubtless the birth we should attribute to *Molloy* is not that of a scholarly composition, but rather the only one that would be suitable to the elusive reality I have been speaking of, that of a myth —

monstrous, and arising from the slumber of reason. There are two analogous truths that can only take shape in us in the form of a myth, these being death and the "absence of humanity" that is death's living semblance. Such absences of reality may not indeed be present in the clear-cut distinctions of discourse, but we may be sure that neither death nor inhumanity, both non-existing, can be considered irrelevant to the existence that we are, of which they are the boundary, the backdrop, and the ultimate truth. Death is not simply that sort of concealed base on which anguish rests: the void into which misery plunges everything, if the latter absorbs us completely and we decompose, is none other than death, object of that horror whose positive aspect is full humanity. Thus this horrible figure painfully swinging along on his crutches is the truth that afflicts us and that follows us no less faithfully than our own shadows: it is fear of this very figure that governs our human gestures, our erect postures and our clear phrases. And, conversely, this figure is in some way the inevitable grave that in the end will draw this parade of humanity into itself to be buried: it is oblivion, impotence. . . . It is not unhappiness, at the end of its strength, that succumbs to misfortune, but rather indifference, in which a man forgets even his own name, perfect indifference to the most loathsome misery. "Yes, there were times when I forgot not only who I was, but that I was, forgot to be." Thus Molloy's thought, or absence of thought, evaporates. . . . And yet this is a bit of chicanery. Molloy or rather the author is *writing*: he is writing and what he writes is that the will to write is slipping away from him. . . . Never mind that he tells us "I have always behaved like a pig." There is not a single human prohibition that has not been swallowed up in an indifference that would like to be definitive and is not, but even being limited to a limping, imperfect indifference, how can one after all not be indifferent? If the author goes back on his decision to "behave like a pig," admits that he has been lying and ends his book with these words: "Then I went back into the house and wrote, It is midnight. The rain is beating on the windows. It was not midnight. It was not raining."—it is simply because he is not Molloy: Molloy would in fact admit *nothing*, because he would write *nothing*.

An author writing while consumed with indifference to what he writes might seem to be acting out a charade; yet is not the mind that discovers this pretense also engaged in pretenses—every bit as fallacious, but with the naïveté of unawareness? The truth, stripped of pretenses, is not to be so easily attained, for before we can attain it we must not only renounce our own pretenses, but forget everything, no longer know anything, be Molloy: an impotent idiot, "not knowing what [he] was going to do until it was done."

All we can do is to set out ourselves in search of Molloy, as does the Jacques Moran of the second part of the book. This character, non-existing as it were, whose dutiful nature and selfish widower's idiosyncracies have something hopeless about them, is the hero of the second part, in which Molloy has disappeared but Moran is sent out to look for him. As though the overwhelming figure of the first part had not sufficiently represented the silence of this world, the impotent search of the second seems to correspond to the need to deliver the universe wholly over to absence, since Molloy is more precisely not to be found than present. But Moran in search of the inaccessible Molloy, slowly stripped of everything, becoming more and more infirm, little by little will be reduced in turn to the same repulsive ambulation as Molloy in the forest.

Thus *literature* necessarily gnaws away at existence and the world, reducing to *nothing* (but this *nothing* is horror) these steps by which we go along confidently from one result to another, from one success to another. This does not exhaust the possibilities available in literature. And it is certain that the use of words for other than utilitarian ends leads in the opposite direction into the domain of rapture, defiance, and gratuitous audacity. But these two realms—horror and rapture—are closer to one another than we have supposed. Would the joys of poetry be accessible to someone who turns away from horror, and would authentic despair be any different from the "golden moment" Molloy experiences at the hands of the police?

Where Now? Who Now?

Maurice Blanchot

Who speaks in Samuel Beckett's books? Who is the tireless "I" who seems always to say the same thing? What are the author's (and the reader's) expectations? — for there must be an author. Or is he trapped in a circuit where he circles blindly, swept along by the flow of stumbling words? Words that are not meaningless but are focusless; that neither start nor stop, and are eager, nevertheless, demanding; and will never stop; nor could we bear them to stop because then we would be faced with the horrifying discovery that when they are not speaking they continue to speak; when they stop they go on; are never silent, for in them silence ceaselessly speaks.

This is a blind alley. Yet the experience carries on, becoming more skeletal from book to book as it discards the few props which enabled it to carry on.

What first strikes us is that here someone is not writing for the worthy purpose of producing a good book. Nor does he write in response to that noble urge we like to call inspiration; or to say the significant things he has to say; or because this is his job; or because he hopes by writing to penetrate into the unknown. Is it then so as to get it over with? Because he is trying to escape from the urge that carries him along by making himself believe that he is still in control and that since he speaks he could just as well stop speaking? What is this vacuum which becomes speech in the inwardness of [him] whom it engulfs? What has he fallen into? "Where now? Who now? When now?"

He is struggling, that is obvious. Sometimes he struggles secretly as though moved by a secret he is hiding from us and even from himself. There is a certain amount of guile in his struggle as well as that other more subtle guile which consists in showing his hand. His first ploy is to put masks and

From *The Sirens' Song*, edited by Gabriel Josipovici. © 1982 by the Harvester Press Ltd.

figures between himself and speech. In *Molloy*, what is expressed still tries to conform to what we think of as a story. But it is not a happy story by any means. Not so much for what it tells—which is wretched—as because it does not manage to tell it. We are well aware that this wanderer deprived even of the wherewithal to wander (though he still has legs and even a bicycle), endlessly circling a mysterious, hidden, revealed and then hidden goal which has something to do with his dead, endlessly dying mother, a goal which, precisely because he has reached it when the book starts ("I am in my mother's room. It's I who live there now") condemns him to a perpetual quest for what obstinately evades him; we are well aware that he is motivated by no ordinary *wanderlust* and that his halting progress takes place in a world which is that of impersonal obsession. Though Molloy is presented to us in bits and pieces he emerges none the less as an identifiable character, a reliable name that protects us from a greater threat. Yet the story has a disturbing tendency to split. It is this tendency, unfulfilled in the wanderer's instability, that requires him finally to split in two, to become someone else, to become Moran, the detective who pursues him without ever overtaking him and who, through his pursuit, becomes just another such eternal wanderer. Molloy turns unawares into Moran, into another, but only into another character, so that the metamorphosis, while not interfering with the reassuring aspect of the story, introduces an allegorical dimension—slightly disappointing, perhaps, in that it is not quite equal to the profound implications it involves.

Malone Dies goes further. Here the wanderer is a dying man and the space he explores has none of the resources still available to *Molloy*: city streets, forests and seascapes. Here there is nothing but a room, a bed and a stick with which the dying man hooks whatever he wants to draw close to him and pushes it away when he no longer wants it, thus extending the range of his forced immobility. There is, too, the pencil which extends his range more significantly since it turns his space into the infinite space of words and stories. Malone, like Molloy, is a name and a face as well as a collection of stories. But the stories are no longer self-supporting. They are not told to convince the reader but as pure, unashamed fictions: "This time I know where I am going. . . . Now it is a game. I am going to play . . . I think I shall be able to tell myself four stories, each one on a different theme." What is the point of these pointless stories? To fill the vacuum into which Malone knows he is falling. Because he dreads all that empty time which will become the endless time of death. To stop this empty time from speaking. And the only way to make it keep quiet is to make it say something, tell a story. So the book is nothing but a way of cheating openly. Whence the creaking compromise which unbalances it, the clash of stratagems thwarting the experience—for stories are only stories. Their brilliance, their sardonic skill, everything which lends them form and interest simultaneously divides them from the dying Malone, divides them from the time of his death to link them to the normal time of stories we do not believe and which, here, do not signify because we are waiting for something much more significant.

In *The Unnamable*, however, the stories do try to stand on their own. The dying Malone had a bed and a room, whereas Mahood is only a derelict stuck in an ornamental jar at the entrance to a restaurant, and Worm has never been born—for him existence consists in a depressing incapacity to exist. And figures from the past, insubstantial phantoms and empty visions, circle mechanically around the vacant centre occupied by the nameless "I." But here all is changed and the experience finds its real depth. These are not people with reassuring individual names, and there is no longer any question of a narrative—not even in the shapeless present of an interior monologue. That which was narrative has now become struggle. That which took shape—albeit tattered and maimed—is here shapeless. Who speaks? Who is the "I" condemned to speak without pause, he who says "I am obliged to speak. I shall never be silent. Never"? A reassuring convention enables us to answer: it is Samuel Beckett. And by doing so we appear to have accepted the awkwardness of a situation which is not fictive but expresses the real tragedy of a real existence; the word experience would refer to something actually experienced. But by so doing we are also trying to reassure ourselves with a name, to situate the book's 'contents' on that personal level where someone is responsible for all that happens in a world where we are spared the ultimate disaster which is to have lost the right to say I. But *The Unnamable* is precisely experience experienced under the threat of impersonality, undifferentiated speech speaking in a vacuum, passing through he who hears it, unfamiliar, excluding the familiar, and which cannot be silenced because it is what is unceasing and interminable.

Who then is speaking? Is it the "author"? But to whom can such a term refer since anyhow he who writes is no longer Beckett but the urge that sweeps him out of himself, turns him into a nameless being, the Unnamable, a being without being who can neither live nor die, stop nor start, who is in the vacant site where speaks the redundancy of idle words under the ill fitting cloak of a porous, agonising I?

Such is the metamorphosis that occurs here. And it is at the heart of this metamorphosis that a speaking relic—the dark residue that refuses to give up—wanders on its motionless journey and struggles, with an endurance that has nothing to do with strength but only with the curse of being unable to stop.

A book deliberately deprived of every support, that elects to begin precisely where there is no possibility of going on and persists stubbornly in staying there, without resorting to trickery or subterfuge and that stumbles on for three hundred pages, advancing not so much as an inch, such a book is undoubtedly worthy of admiration. But this is only an outsider's view, that of the reader contemplating what strikes him as a tour de force. There is little to be admired in an accomplishment which cannot be avoided. Nothing which calls for admiration in the fact of being imprisoned and of going round and round in a space from which even death will not extricate you—because to be there required first being outside life. Aesthetic considerations are out of place here. Perhaps what we have before us is not a book because it is more than a book. It is a direct confrontation with the process from which all books derive—with the original point at which the work is inevitably lost, that always destroys the work, recreates endless idleness in the work, but with which too, if anything is to come of it, an ever more primal relationship has to be established. The Unnamable is indeed condemned to drain the cup of infinity:

> I have nothing to do, that is to say nothing in particular. I have to speak, whatever that means. Having nothing to say, no words but the words of others, I have to speak. No one compels me to, there is no one, it's an accident, a fact. Nothing can ever exempt me from it, there is nothing, nothing to discover, nothing to recover, nothing to lessen what remains to say, I have the ocean to drink, so there is an ocean then.

How did it happen? Sartre has shown how literature, by expressing the deep-rooted "evil" that beset Genet, gradually endowed him with craftsmanship and power, raising him from passivity to a purposeful prose:

> This work [*Our Lady of Flowers*] is, without the author's suspecting it, the journal of a detoxication, of a conversion. In it Genet detoxicates himself of himself and turns to the outside world. In fact, this book *is* detoxication itself. . . . Born of a nightmare, it affects—line by line, page by page, from death to life, from the state of dream to that of waking, from madness to sanity—a passageway that is marked with relapses.
>
> (J.-P. Sartre, *Saint Genet*)

By infecting us, says Sartre, Genet cures himself. Each of his books is a crisis of cathartic possession, a psychodrama. Superficially, each one seems to be a repetition of that which precedes it, yet with each, this possessed being acquires a little more control over the demon that possesses him.

This is not an entirely unfamiliar view of creative experience. It is expressed in the conventional interpretation of Goethe's "Poetry is deliverance." *Les Chants de Maldoror* might also be seen as illustrating it with its forceful metaphors, passionate images and obsessive repetitions that conjure up from darkest night and by means of darkness itself a new being who seeks his true image in the light of day, whence emerges Lautréamont. But it would be wrong to imagine that when literature seems to lead into daylight it leads to the peaceful enjoyment of rational clarity. The passion for ordinary daylight which, in Lautréamont, is raised to the dangerous heights of banality, together with his passion for ordinary speech that becomes self-destructive through a sarcastic indulgence in cliché and pastiche, makes him lose himself in the boundlessness of a daylight which eclipses him. And as Sartre rightly observes, if for Genet, too, literature appears to open a way and make self-control possible, he discovers, once success has been achieved, that suddenly there is no way that can be his way; or discovers the total failure of a success that is no more than a meaningless academic career. At the time of *Our Lady* the poem was the way. But once he had woken up, had no cause to worry about the future, nothing to fear, there was no longer any reason to write. He did not want to become a "writer." It seems obvious that a man whose work responds to such an instinctive urge, whose style is a weapon fashioned by so exact an intention, whose every image and theory so manifestly epitomise his whole life, cannot suddenly begin to talk about something else. The loser wins: achieving the status of writer he loses at one go the need, the wish, the occasion and the means to write.

There is also, of course, the conventional image of literary creativity where the writer is happily freed from the darker side of his nature by a work that transforms it as though by magic into the characteristic joy and lightheartedness of this work and where the writer finds relief, or even the realisation of his lonely personality in free communication with others. That is what Freud believed when he stressed the virtues of sublimation with an endearing confidence in the powers of consciousness and self-expression. But things are not always so simple, and it must be admitted that there is another side to the experience which exasperated Michaelangelo's despair and Goya's obsession, drove happy-go-lucky Gerard de Nerval round the bend and led Hölderlin to be swept away in the tide of poetic progress.

How does this occur? We can only suggest two areas of investigation.

First that art is not for those who see it as a barrier behind which they can retreat peacefully into themselves, sheltered from everyday preoccupations. For although they may think they are thus protected from reality they are in fact exposed to a more serious danger for which they are totally unprepared: the threat of alienation, because they are alienated. And this is a threat they must not avoid but indulge. Art requires that he who practises it should be immolated to art, should become other, not another, not transformed from the human being he was into an artist with artistic duties, satisfactions and interests, but into nobody, the empty, animated space where art's summons is heard.

But why should art require this metamorphosis? It could be said that this is because, since it cannot take off from the trodden path, it seeks what has not yet been thought, heard or seen. But such an answer seems to leave out the main point. It could further be said that it is because artistic creation deprives the artist—the living person, living in a community where he is in contact with reality, where he relies on the consistency of things done and to be done, and where he participates, whether he likes it or not, in the reality of the common scheme—deprives him of reality by forcing him to dwell in the world of imaginary things. And indeed what *The Unnamable* depicts is this malaise of one who has dropped out of reality and drifts forever in the gap between existence and nothingness, incapable of dying and incapable of being born, haunted by the phantoms he creates, in which he does not believe and which refuse to communicate with him. But neither is this the whole answer. The whole answer should rather be found in the process by which the work of art, seeking its realisation, constantly reverts to the point where it is confronted with failure. The point where language ceases to speak but is, where nothing begins, nothing is said, but where language is always reborn and always starts afresh.

It is this exploration of the origins that makes artistic creation such a risky undertaking—both for the artist and for art. But this exploration is also the one thing that makes art an important activity. And it is because *The Unnamable* makes us realise this in the bluntest possible way that it is more important than most of the "successful" books published. Let us try to hear this voice that speaks knowing that it is lying, indifferent to what it says, too old perhaps and too humiliated to be able ever to say the words that would make it stop. And let us try to do down to the world into which sinks, henceforth condemned to speak, he who in order that he may write dwells in a timelessness where he must die in an endless dying:

> The words are everywhere, inside me, outside me, well, well a
> minute ago I had no thickness, I hear them, no need to hear them,

no need of a head, impossible to stop them, impossible to stop.
I'm in words, made of words, others' words, what others, the
place too, the air, the walls, the floor, the ceiling, all words, the
whole world is here with me, I'm the air, the walls, the walled-
in one, everything yields, opens, ebbs, flows, like flakes. I'm all
these flakes, meeting, mingling, falling asunder, wherever I go
I find me, leave me, go towards me, come from me, nothing ever
but me, a particle of me, retrieved, lost, gone astray, I'm all these
words, all these strangers, this dust of words, with no ground
for their settling, no sky for their dispersing, coming together
to say, fleeing one another to say, that I am they, all of them,
those that merge, those that part, those that never meet, and
nothing else, yes, something else, that I'm something else quite
different, a quite different thing, a wordless thing in an empty
place, a hard, shut, dry, cold, black space, where nothing stirs,
nothing speaks, and that I listen, and that I seek, like a caged
beast born of caged beasts born of caged beasts born of caged beasts.

The Trilogy

Hugh Kenner

MOLLOY

Molloy begins, "I am in my mother's room." That is clear enough. "It's I who live there now." Also clear. "I don't know how I got there." Succinct. And so on: short sentences setting forth the elements of his present state, in which he writes out a statement for which, delivered in installments, a man comes every week. It's not clear who wants it, or why, nor why they (it is "they," a kind of tolerant Gestapo) are displeased with the way he began it. "Here's my beginning," he tells us. "Here it is." There ensues an unbroken unparagraphed narrative, nothing but easy chronological flow, some hundred pages of it. Its sentences are not staccato but long and easy, elegiac, and it transports us without effort into uncertainties like those of the world of *Watt*. "It is in the tranquility of decomposition that I remember the long confused emotion which was my life," and confusion is certainly the norm of its simplest episodes, suffused though they are by the ceremony of leavetaking, for Molloy will not be thinking of them again.

> This time, then once more I think, then perhaps a last time, then I think it'll be over, with that world too. Premonition of the last but one but one. All grows dim. A little more and you'll grow blind. It's in the head. It doesn't work any more, it says, I don't work any more. You go dumb as well and sounds fade. The threshold scarcely crossed that's how it is. It's the head. It must have had enough. So that you say, I'll manage this time, then perhaps once more, then perhaps a last time, then nothing more.

From *A Reader's Guide to Samuel Beckett.* © 1973 by Thames & Hudson Ltd. Farrar, Straus & Giroux, 1973.

"You go dumb as well and sounds fade": Vergil has no finer cadence, no juxtaposition more sensitive to rhythms and vowels. There is more sustained emotion in the first half of *Molloy* than in anything else Beckett has written. "Cows were chewing in enormous fields, lying and standing, in the evening silence." How soothing are these cows, fixed in that amber cadence. How soothing, too, the elusively neutral landscape.

> From there he must have seen it all, the plain, the sea, and then these selfsame hills that some call mountains, indigo in places in the evening light, their serried ranges crowding to the skyline, cloven with hidden valleys that the eye divines from sudden shifts of colour and then from other signs for which there are no words, nor even thoughts.

These are last looks, last thoughts; "If you think of the forms and light of other days it is without regret," and yet "what magic in those dim things to which it will be time enough, when next they pass, to say goodbye."

The emotion is sure, the events are as far from sureness as the events of *Watt*, though not from paucity of data (to be interrogated with fierce attention) but from uncertainty of memory (to be accepted, though often to be regretted). He recalls a kind of archetypal event, a meeting, observed by him from high up above that wide landscape: A and C meeting on an evening walk. They have left the town separately, one has turned back, they meet, exchange words inaudible at this great distance. Are they strangers or not? Then they go their ways, C onward, A back toward the town, and Molloy speculates first on the one who is going onward, "innocent, greatly innocent, he had nothing to fear, though he went in fear, he had nothing to fear, there was nothing they could do to him, or very little. But he can't have known it. . . . Yes, he saw himself threatened, his body threatened, his reason threatened, and perhaps he was, perhaps they were, in spite of his innocence. What business has innocence here? What relation to the innumerable spirits of darkness?" That is perhaps an Occupation note, though it need not be; it applies quite as well to normal times. (The novel was written about 1947.) And as to the one who is going back toward town, Molloy forgets by now if he is A or C, but speculates about him likewise, noting that he moved "with a kind of loitering indolence which rightly or wrongly seemed to me expressive." That sounds like a line from a detective novel, as indeed does the whole business of Molloy's surveillance of A and C, and his speculations about them. (Camier, incidentally, it emerges almost casually part way through *Mercier et Camier*, is a private detective.) But then Molloy starts to wonder if he is perhaps confusing several different occasions, "And perhaps it was A one day at one place, then C another at another, then a third the rock and I, and so on for the other components, the cows, the sky, the sea, the mountains. I can't believe it. No, I will not lie, I can easily conceive it. No matter, no matter, let us go on." And, a little later, "A and C I never saw again."

Not that we do not wonder whether one or another of the various people he does subsequently meet may be A or C, a meaningless question come to think of it, since whatever may be the case in real life, one character in a novel is identical with another character in a novel only if the author somehow, overtly or covertly, asserts that he is. But for the time being no author is in sight except Molloy. It is like this novel to play on our tendency to forget that we are reading a piece of writing, and also to remind us periodically of that fact. For the reader's uncertainties cannot surpass Molloy's, nor Molloy's the reader's. Molloy is Beckett's first venture in a new kind of character, what he once called in a letter "the narrator/narrated." It is a device he employs in all his subsequent fiction, bringing the ambient world into existence only so far as the man holding the pencil can remember it or understand it, so that no omniscient craftsman is holding anything back, and simultaneously bringing into existence the man with the pencil, who is struggling to create himself, so to speak, by recalling his own past or delineating his own present. As *Watt* was a step beyond *Murphy*, and *Mercier et Camier* a hesitant step beyond *Watt*, so this is a further step, into uncharted, foreordained terrain. The business of filling the air with uncertainty, the uncertainty fiction normally dissipates, need no longer be left to style, style being now identical with the uncertain mental processes of a protagonist.

The outline of Molloy's story is deceptively simple. After seeing A and C out of sight, he resolves to go and see his mother. There is no reason for this resolve, moreover he hates her, but the purpose consumes him. He sets off on his bicycle. He falls foul of the police, also for no reason. This episode establishes the extent to which he and officialdom inhabit totally different worlds, so that neither has the faintest grasp of what the other is saying. He meets a woman named Mrs Lousse as a result of running over her dog, and is kept in her house for a while at her behest, it is unclear why. He leaves there on his crutches, abandoning the bicycle; loses interest in his mother and leaves town; is attracted by his mother again and attempts to find town again; and beset by steady physical disintegration (stiffening of his good leg, shortening of a leg, loss of toes, loss of strength, arthritis in wrists) he wanders, then crawls, then lies immobile in a ditch. He has heard a voice, which may be hallucinatory: "Don't fret Molloy, we're coming." He does not fret. He does not even wish. "Molloy could stay, where he happened to be."

Such an outline, it is clear, conveys little; the events are unimportant. What is important (a word to be used with diffidence) is the look of aimlessness itself, the degeneration, then, of purpose into crawling, the degeneration of body into physical wreckage, and the degeneration of the lyricism that observed A and C and their landscape into a savage and prickly distaste for all phenomena, not excluding self and not excluding language. For instance,

> But I also said, Yet a little while, at the rate things are going, and I won't be able to move, but will have to stay, where I happen to be, unless someone comes and carries me. Oh I did not say it in such limpid language. And when I say I said, etc., all I mean is that I knew confusedly things were so, without knowing exactly what it was all about. And every time I say, I said this, or, I said that, or speak of a voice saying, far away inside me, Molloy, and then a fine phrase more or less clear and simple, or find myself compelled to attribute to others intelligible words, or hear my own voice uttering to others more or less articulate sounds, I am merely complying with the convention that demands you either lie or hold your peace.

The world grows slowly sour, grows infected, grows repellent. Nevertheless the mind will not be still, and working away amid phenomena it has no taste for it, it achieves without laughing an ever blacker, ever wilder comedy.

> And I even crawled on my back, plunging my crutches blindly behind me into the thickets, and with the black boughs for sky to my closing eyes. I was on my way to mother. And from time to time I said, Mother, to encourage me I suppose. I kept losing my hat, the lace had broken long ago, until in a fit of temper I banged it down on my skull with such violence that I couldn't get it off again. And if I had met any lady friends, if I had any lady friends, I would have been powerless to salute them correctly.

Imagine, in such a pass, thinking of saluting ladies correctly! Imagine, for that matter, being human: which is what *Molloy*, in its fashion, incites us to do.

At this point a new narrator takes up a new tale. "My name is Moran, Jacques. That is the name I am known by. I am done for. My son too. All unsuspecting. He must think he's on the threshold of life, of real life. He's right there. His name is Jacques, like mine. This cannot lead to confusion."

He is right in rejecting an identity of names as a source of confusion, but wrong if he supposes there will be no confusion, for into confusion, of Molloy's inimitable kind, Moran sinks: that is the substance of his narrative.

Molloy, on the second page of his narrative, had speculated whether he had a son. "But I think not. He would be old now, nearly as old as myself. . . . It seems to me sometimes that I even knew my son, that I helped him. Then I tell myself it's impossible." The fact that both narrators' names begin with Mo is the first similarity between them. The turning of the narrative toward a son is the second; and as Moran's tale proceeds the similarities multiply. They are even both capable of lyricism about bicycles. Moran, it would seem, is like an earlier stage of Molloy, telling the tale of how he began a good bourgeois, parish prist and all, and became a bum. Molloy's tale is of how a bum became a casualty, and it has even been suggested that Molloy is Moran, a later stage of Moran, and that the two parts of the novel have been transposed from their chronological order, the whole tracing one man's descent from garden and wicker chair to utter alienation. This suggestion contains a truth, that Moran at the end of his episode is as disoriented as Molloy at the beginning of his, but it is nevertheless surely false since it reduces Beckett's most powerful effect to the level of a trick. For the eerie power of the book arises surely from the mysterious hold of Molloy, whom he has never seen, on Moran's imagination, and the mysterious psychic disintegration that is perhaps a consequence of this hold, or perhaps its accidental concomitant. It is as though preoccupation with Molloy has power to make the familiar liaisons with familiar reality dissolve; as though Molloy is rather a myth than a character, with a myth's hold on its believers.

As, during his surveillance of A and C, we might have mistaken Molloy for a detective, so at the beginning of Moran's narrative we are entitled on much better evidence to think of him as an operative of some kind. A certain Gaber comes and gives him instructions, reads them to him in fact, but does not suffer him to retain them in written form. This is routine. We do not hear these instructions, but it is evident that the Organization, small or large Moran does not know, has enjoined him to find Molloy. Molloy is surely not worth anyone's trouble, but this is not gone into. (In Occupied France many persons were being sought who were not on the face of it worth anyone's trouble.)

Gaber is "a messenger." The Greek for "messenger" is *angelos*, and the name of a well-known angel is Gabriel. We shall do well to make little of this. Like the hints of detective-story format, it is one of Beckett's devices for imparting to the narrative a sense of near-familiarity, near-intelligibility. To hint at numerous patterns that do not really fit, that will certainly not fit the way the *Odyssey* can be fitted to *Ulysses*, is a device among many for installing us in a world that dissolves. It resembles the inconsequence into which paragraphs lapse, with no loss of grip on the rigorous local clarity of terms and sentences, or the arbitrariness that characterizes Moran's actions just when we are beginning to suppose that we understand them and him.

No sooner has "the Molloy affair" begun than Moran's self-control is faltering. Within a few pages he is making plans out of their proper order ("I was losing my head already"); two more pages and he is receiving communion without having properly fasted, compromising as he does so his disagreeable piety (he is a loveless man) in a manner expressive of how much he is by now contriving to shut out of his mind. The dialogue with the priest is wonderfully perfunctory:

> It's this, I said, Sunday for me without the Body and Blood is like—. He raised his hand. Above all no profane comparisons, he said. Perhaps he was thinking of the kiss without a moustache or beef without mustard. I dislike being interrupted. I sulked. Say no more, he said, a wink is as good as a nod, you want communion. I bowed my head. It's a little unusual, he said. I wondered if he had fed. I knew he was given to prolonged fasts, by way of mortification certainly, and then because his doctor advised it. Thus he killed two birds with one stone. Not a word to a soul, he said, let it remain between us and—. He broke off, raising a finger, and his eyes, to the ceiling. Heavens, he said, what is that stain? I looked in turn at the ceiling. Damp, I said. Tut tut, he said, how annoying. The words tut tut seemed to me the maddest I had heard. There are times, he said, when one feels like weeping.

And communion is given and received in the following spirit:

> He came back with a kind of portable pyx, opened it and despatched me without an instant's hesitation. I rose and thanked him warmly. Pah! he said, it's nothing. Now we can talk.

Such is Moran, or such at any rate is Moran within an hour of having heard of Molloy. He abuses his son—this appears to be routine, he does it so often to so little protest. They set out; his instructions begin to fade in his mind, not long after he has told us with the confidence of habit that he will be able to recover their minutest details at will; he undergoes leg pains; loses son, bicycle and money; is reduced to lying on the ground, and crawling; is summoned home, to find his bees and hens dead, his house deserted; and as we take our leave of him he is preparing to set out into the world on crutches ("Perhaps I shall meet Molloy"). His health is now approximately

Molloy's health when Molloy began his own quest; the end of the novel thus nearly joins the beginning.

There are other oddities. He meets a man with a heavy coat and a striking hat and a stick, who corresponds, as far as these details go, with the man Molloy sighted so long ago and denominated C, the man who set out "alone, by unknown ways, in the gathering night, with a stick." Is it C? We cannot say. If it is C, then C has surely disintegrated too, for the man Moran meets has "a huge shock of dirty snow-white hair," and begs for bread. On the other hand, we have no assurance that C, when Molloy saw him, would not have displayed such hair had he taken off his hat; we have only, from Molloy, the impression of C's well-groomed self-possession. For that matter, the man Moran meets somewhat resembles his anticipation of Molloy, "hirsute, craggy and grimacing." It is Molloy? But we have no reason to suppose that Moran's anticipation of Molloy is accurate, nor have we any record of Molloy's encountering anyone who resembles Moran.

Not long afterward Moran meets a man who resembles himself, enquiring after an old man with a stick. Is it the same old man? And is this another operative like Moran himself, not yet disintegrated? Is this perhaps even A? He kills this man. It is the most perfunctory killing in literature, occurring as it does in the interval between two sentences. "He thrust his hand at me. . . . I do not know what happened then. But a little later, perhaps a long time later, I found him stretched on the ground, his head in a pulp. I am sorry I cannot indicate more clearly how this result was obtained, it would have been something worth reading."

This is a valuable emblem of the book. There is never an obscure sentence. Absolute precision, absolute, almost finicky certainty attends the grip of these sentences upon meaning. And yet the uncertainties occur, and pervade, as a house might be in a state of dilapidation without one beam sagging nor one post crumpled. And if we inspect the opening and the closing sentences of Moran's report, the dilapidation of the intervening structure appears nearly absolute. His narrative begins, "It is midnight. The rain is beating on the windows. I am calm. All is sleeping. Nevertheless I get up and go to my desk." The narrative ends. "Then I went back into the house and wrote, It is midnight. The rain is beating on the windows. It was not midnight. It was not raining."

MALONE DIES

"Malone," writes Malone, "is what I am called now." Some pages later he indicates that "the Murphys, Merciers, Molloys, Morans, Malones" were all beings of his devising. He created, he killed. "How many have I killed, hitting them on the head or setting fire to them?" He manages to think of five, who would include Murphy and the retired butler in *Murphy*; the *agent* in *Mercier et Camier*; the enquirer killed by Moran, and the charcoal-burner assaulted by Molloy, both in *Molloy* (assuming, that is, that the charcoal-burner died, for we have no testimony to this). Malone is now dying himself, and whiling away the time as before with stories. He calls himself an octogenarian, and speaks of having lived thirty thousand odd days, which would make him at least eighty-two. His plan for the narrative he is starting to write, sitting in bed in an obscure place with an exercise-book and a pencil, is to describe his present state, to tell himself four — on reconsideration, three — stories, to inventory his possessions, to die. His death and the end of his narrative will necessarily synchronize. The fact that he will not be able to describe his death becomes, however, a paradigmatic fact, for he is unable to carry out any other element of the plan. The account of his present state is intermittent, elusive and contradictory, the stories telescope into one, or possibly two, and the inventory of his possessions, a luxury he promises himself, occurs prematurely ("Quick quick my possessions") and seems not to be completed, the expected pleasure of numerate certainty dwindling into distracted quibbles. The book ends as he is slaughtering the characters in his story. Is he himself dead? Is some remoter author slaughtering him? Has he merely lost strength, or interest, not life? But he has no life, never had; he is simply the person we intuit when a hundred or more pages of highly idiosyncratic words claim that a person is behind them. For words always make such a claim. Where else would they come from, if not from a person?

It is clear that *Molloy* and *Malone Dies* were conceived as companion books. "*Cette fois-ci, puis encore une je pense, puis c'en sera fini je pense,*" runs the opening of Molloy's narrative in the French edition published in 1951, and *Malone Meurt* was published in the same year. "This time, then once more I think, then I think it'll be over." It was two years later that *L'Innommable* appeared, to make the trilogy, and when the English *Molloy* was published in 1955 Beckett revised this sentence to entail not two but three tellings. This appears to mean that though *L'Innommable* existed in manuscript in 1951, Beckett had either not decided whether he would publish it, or at any rate not decided whether the three books made a trilogy, though he had long known that the first two made a duet.

It is helpful, at any rate, for the reader of *Malone Dies* to bear *Molloy* in mind, since the analogy between the two will keep his attention focussed on dualities of structure, and both books work by dividings into two. As *Molloy* is divided between Molloy's and Moran's consciousness and between their consecutive narratives, so different to start with yet so oddly convergent, *Malone Dies* alternates between Malone's "present state" (always shifting, because days pass) and the story he is amusing himself with; and the two, though they start quite differently, also converge, so that the hero of the story is eventually as old as Malone and confined to a similar room. The story, moreover, is itself twofold, the hero having apparently changed names part way, from Sapo (*homo sapiens*) to Macmann (son of man), as it were by analogy with Molloy and Malone.

Sapo, properly Saposcat (Gk. *skatos*, of or concerning dung) is a frigid brat, boring to his creator ("What tedium", subjoins Malone after only two paragraphs). "He was the eldest child of poor and sickly parents," and we are treated to a long paragraph on their poor and sickly aspirations. Saposcat *père* might get more money working longer hours, but lacks the strength. They might obviate the need for thoughts about more money by growing vegetables, but need manure, which costs money they do not have. "Nothing remained but to envisage a smaller house. But we are cramped as it is, said Mrs Saposcat. And it was an understood thing that they would be more and more so with every passing year until the day came when, the departure of the first-born compensating the arrival of the new-born, a kind of equilibrium would be attained. Then little by little the house would empty. And at last they would be all alone, with their memories. It would be time enough then to move. He would be pensioned off, she at her last gasp. They would take a cottage in the country where, having no further need of manure, they could afford to buy it in cartloads. And their children, grateful for the sacrifices made on their behalf, would come to their assistance. It was in this atmosphere of unbridled dream that these conferences usually ended. It was as though the Saposcats drew the strength to live from the prospect of their impotence."

As for little Sapo, "At least his health is good, said Mr Saposcat. Not all that, said his wife. But no definite disease, said Mr Saposcat. A nice thing that would be, at his age, said his wife." "What tedium," indeed. Yet Sapo, though a simpleton who cannot tell one bird or one tree from another, soon shows signs of acquiring a life of his own. When he commits a fault that would merit expulsion from school and yet is not expelled, Malone breaks off to remark that he has not been able to find out why Sapo was not expelled, quite as if Sapo had resources that are hidden from the man who seems to be making him up. That is no doubt why Malone continues to recount the fortunes of Sapo; Sapo, who started out by being a puppet, now possesses the fascinations of autonomy. If you are amusing yourself with a fictional character you do not advance the excitement by making him remain motionless, often standing, for hours on end; but if you *encounter* a boy who behaves like that, even if you encounter him in your thoughts, then he is not without a certain allure. "People wondered what he could brood on thus, hour by hour," and Malone seems to be wondering too.

> His father supposed him a prey to the first flutterings of sex. At sixteen I was the same, he would say. At sixteen you were earning your living, said his wife. So I was, said Mr Saposcat. But in the view of his teachers the signs were rather those of besottedness pure and simple. Sapo dropped his jaw and breathed through his mouth. It is not easy to see in virtue of what this expression is incompatible with erotic thoughts. But indeed his dream was less of girls than of himself, his own life, his life to be. That is more than enough to stop up the nose of a lucid and sensitive boy, and cause his jaw temporarily to sag.

"We are getting on," comments Malone. "Nothing is less like me than this patient, reasonable child, struggling all alone for years to shed a little light upon himself, avid of the last gleam, a stranger to the joys of darkness. Here truly is the air I needed, a lively tenuous air, far from the nourishing murk that is killing me." He introduces more characters, the Lamberts, equally devoid of charm. Big Lambert is a pig-sticker by vocation, and his evening conversation ("to his near and dear ones, while the lamp burned low") is solely of the last pig he has slaughtered. The only reported utterances of his overworked wife are "angry unanswerable questions, such as, What's the use?" Sapo lingers among them, silent, unnoticed, staring, as though turning into an illiterate Murphy. He watches their incompetent burial of a mule. ("Together they dragged the mule by the legs to the edge of the hole and heaved it in, on its back. The forelegs, pointing towards heaven, projected above the level of the ground. Old Lambert banged them down with his spade.") There is little incident, little interest, and yet a thread of tenuous interest holds Malone: the thought of Sapo, who could not glide away "because his movements were rather those of one floundering in a quag," the thought of Sapo, awkward and bizarre, pausing to stare down at the earth, "blind to its beauty, and to its utility, and to the little wild many-coloured flowers happy among the crops and weeds." This thought draws Malone back to his own boyhood, and to an evocation of remembered sounds:

> Then in my bed, in the dark, on stormy nights, I could tell one from another, in the outcry without, the leaves, the boughs, the groaning trunks, even the grasses and the house that sheltered

me. Each tree has its own cry, just as no two whispered alike,
when the air was still. . . . The sound I liked best had nothing
noble about it. It was the barking of the dogs, at night, in the
clusters of hovels up in the hills, where the stone-cutters lived,
like generations of stone-cutters before them. It came down to
me where I lay, in the house in the plain, wild and soft, at the
limit of earshot, soon weary. The dogs of the valley replied with
their gross bay all fangs and jaws and foam.

This is, as distinct from the paragraphs that synthesize Sapo, a flow of genuine
sap, tapped deep down where his most real feelings are buried. Feeling is
buried very deep in Malone, and it is fascinating to watch its sudden eloquence, stirred as if by accident. The self on top now is the self of a loveless
old man, but he has not quite killed deeper selves. That is perhaps one meaning of the title: his life has been a long dying, not yet terminated, of a boy
once fully alive there.

There is sometimes an incident, as when he loses his pencil. There is
sometimes another, as when he loses his stick. ("That is the outstanding event
of the day." What days!) Even this loss yields more than we'd think. He
lost it trying to wield it like a punt-pole, to propel his bed on its casters
(if it has any) through the door "and even down the stairs, if there is a stairs
that goes down." That is like a boy's fantasy. The man's part is to meditate
on the stick, like Swift meditating on a broomstick. "It is thus that man
distinguishes himself from the ape and rises, from discovery to discovery,
ever higher, towards the light": there is no mistaking the sardonic bitterness
of this estimate of the man's mature estate. Another incident: a man comes
in, hits him on the head to waken him, then stands by his bed unspeaking
for seven hours, with a break for lunch. This is human fellowship, so far
as we are shown it. Malone draws up a list of twenty-one written questions
in case the man returns, but he does not.

The lights fade and shift, the room seems to alter, certainly his body alters.

All strains towards the nearest deeps, and notably my feet, which
even in the ordinary way are so much further from me than all
the rest, from my head I mean, for that is where I am fled, my
feet are leagues away. And to call them in, to be cleaned for example, would I think take me over a month, exclusive of the time
required to locate them. Strange, I don't feel my feet any more,
my feet feel nothing any more, and a mercy it is. And yet I feel
they are beyond the range of the most powerful telescope. Is that
what is known as having a foot in the grave?

But more important than any of these "present state" happenings, the story gathers momentum. Sapo wanders off and is found by his creator ("I have taken a long time to find him again, but I have found him. How did I know it was he, I don't know.") A good question, since even his name has changed; he is now Macmann, son of Man, an aged wanderer, even as Molloy. He is telling himself a story, "the kind of story he has been telling himself all his life, saying, This cannot possibly last much longer." So his growing resemblance to Malone is unmistakable. Then he passes out of sight rolling, like Molloy crawling; comes to in "a kind of asylum" (is that the kind of place Malone is now?); then — O wonder! — he undergoes a love story, for his place of repose is peopled, as Malone's seems not to be.

The lady is Moll, another inmate, "immoderately ill-favoured of both face and body." There springs up gradually between her and Macmann, we are told, a kind of intimacy, of which they attempt a physical translation. But, "given their age and scant experience of carnal love, it was natural that they should not succeed, at first shot, in giving each other the impression that they were made for each other." Nevertheless, "far from losing heart, they warmed to their work. And though both were completely impotent they finally succeeded, summoning to their aid all the resources of the skin, the mucus and the imagination, in striking from their dry and feeble clips a kind of sombre gratification. So that Moll exclaimed, being (at that stage) the more expansive of the two, Oh would we had but met sixty years ago! But on the long road to this what flutterings, alarms and bashful fumblings, of which only this, that they gave Macmann some insight into the meaning of the expression, Two is company."

This is one more of the resonant passages. From beneath the wilful grotesquerie of his fiction, the buried Malone, the Malone of feeling, is nearly breaking forth. "In striking from their dry and feeble clips a kind of sombre gratification": Beckett has nowhere any finer sentence, though many as fine. It is no sombre gratification that such language yields; its clips, far from dry and feeble, touch on noble resources of eloquence, Vergilian in their amber evocation of the sorrowful, the futile, the ever-hopeful. And that is the peculiarity of this book, in contrast with *Molloy*, that it rises to such extraordinary heights. At best the feeling in *Molloy* is mellow, elegiac. Malone is capable of starker rages, more conscious wit, and more impressive peaks. "Two is company," a seeming tautology, is human wisdom, the meaning of which each man must discover, if at all, for himself. Sardonic though the pedantry with which he quotes it, Malone is heartbreakingly close, at such times, to the liberty that comports with such understanding.

Malone, though, has he ever gained insight into the meaning of this expression? We cannot say. More to the point, we cannot tell that he has not. His company, here, now, is perforce mental: Macmann, Moll, sundry lunatics, a Lady Pedal who enjoins the lunatics in the story to "Sing! Make the most of this glorious day!" and a Lemuel who goes about at the end dispatching them with a hatchet, for no reason except that Malone seems tired of them. Malone's possessions included a photograph concerning which he worked up some delicacies of feeling.

> It is not a photograph of me, but I am perhaps at hand. It is an ass, taken from in front and close up, at the edge of the ocean, it is not the ocean, but for me it is the ocean. They naturally tried to make it raise its head, so that its beautiful eyes might be impressed on the celluloid, but it holds it lowered. You can tell by its ears that it is not pleased. They put a boater on its head. The thin hard parallel legs, the little hooves light and dainty on the sand. The outline is blurred, that's the operator's giggle shaking the camera.

These are cautious affections that Malone is indulging. Turning his attention to his story, he reflects, "Moll, I'm going to kill her." He does. In the story she dies, not without undergoing a loss of hair such that "she confessed to Macmann that she did not dare comb it any more, for fear of making it fall out even faster. He said to himself with satisfaction, She tells me everything." And a photograph survives her. Are we to connect this photograph, Malone's fantasy, with the photograph of the ass, which he really possessed, and with his evident affection for "the little hooves light and dainty on the sand"?

> Macmann carried with him and contemplated from time to time the photograph that Moll had given him. . . . She was standing beside a chair and squeezing in her hands her long plaits. Traces were visible, behind her, of a kind of trellis with clambering flowers. . . . When giving this keep-sake to Macmann she had said, I was fourteen, I well remember the day, a summer day, it was my birthday, afterwards they took me to see Punch and Judy. . . . Diligently Moll pressed her lips together, in order to hide her great buck-teeth. The roses must have been pretty, they must have scented the air. In the end Macmann tore up this photograph and threw the bits in the air, one windy day. Then they scattered, though all subjected to the same conditions, as though with alacrity.

Why does Macmann tear up the photograph? We may perhaps reflect that he never knew *that* Moll. We may also reflect that he is a projection of his author, Malone, he of "I'm going to kill her." And kill everyone else he does, so far as he can, within ten more pages; and the last words are,

> never anything
>
> there
>
> any more

How loveless is Malone, how dryly jaunty, how miserable, how funny. The man who conceived the notion of poling his bed down the stairs has a claim on our sympathies, as congeners of Columbus and Galileo, that one would never predict from his misanthropies alone. He is one of the most engaging of the Beckett twilight men. The book has not a dull page, not even when its subject is dullness, and we nearly do not notice how the lethal rages that shake the man before us bespeak a quiescent monster who was long ago otherwise.

THE UNNAMABLE

The Unnamable—so named because, at the simplest level of meaning, he does not know who he may be and hopes to find out—sits nowhere, nowhen, "like a great horned owl in an aviary," grinding his "wordy-gurdy." "I am in my mother's room," began Molloy. "Where now?" begins the newest voice.

> Can it be . . . that one day I simply stayed in, in where, instead of going out, in the old way, out to spend day and night as far away as possible, it wasn't far. Perhaps that is how it began. You think you are simply resting the better to act when the time comes, and you soon find yourself powerless ever to do anything again. No matter how it happened. I say it, not knowing what.

That is as much of an explanation as we are going to get. One can imagine Murphy, one day, simply staying in. But the pure bliss of Murphy was banished from Beckett's cosmos long ago, as was the reader's pure bliss which entails knowing exactly what is happening and just who did what to whom. For the explanation that has been provisionally offered, that we are hearing from a man who formerly went out but one day simply decided to stay in, will fade very quickly as many multiplied words make his situation more and more mysterious and distressing. Thus shortly he is talking of the compulsion to string out words, likening it to a pensum, an imposition of lines to be written out as a punishment for inaccurately repeating a lesson. Yet he does not know what lines he is to write out, and can only hope to hit on the right ones by chance. And when he has completed the pensum he will still have the lesson to repeat, and will have to rely on chance to get that right also. "Strange notion in any case, and eminently open to suspicion, that of a task to be performed, before one can be at rest. Strange task, which consists in speaking of oneself. Strange hope, turned towards silence and peace."

All this is provisional, hypothetical; yet, he says, "Let us suppose . . . that it is in fact required of me that I say something that is not to be found in all I have said up to now." "All I have said up to now" includes the previous fictions of Samuel Beckett. "All these Murphys, Molloys and Malones do not fool me. They have made me waste my time, suffer for nothing, speak of them when, in order to stop speaking, I should have spoken of me and me alone." For the goal is to stop speaking. We are veering close to the Gestapo theme: the theme of the man who is required to talk, and in fact does not possess the information his tormentors must be made to think they have extracted. They will leave him alone, he may conjecture, if he has the aplomb for conjecture, when by accident he hits on something plausible.

> When all goes silent, and comes to an end, it will be because the words have been said, those it behoved me to say, no need to know which, no means of knowing which, they'll be there somewhere, in the heap, in the torrent, not necessarily the last, they have to be ratified by the proper authority, that takes time, he's far from here, they bring him the verbatim report of the proceedings, once in a way, he knows the words that count.

And while word goes back and forth to the proper authority, the monologue must necessarily go on. Perhaps the requisite words have already been spoken? If so, how long will it be before the speaker knows?

Still less than *Godot*, though, is this an "Occupation" book, for the writer's impulse to write is another of its themes, a mysterious theme, and everyone's impulse to talk, and the need of the mind to remain in action whether it has anything to engage it or not. We have thoughts *of* something; we also have thoughts that find something to be about, many things successively to be about, as in the "stream of consciousness." And again, there is thought that barely ticks over, like an idling motor, propelling nothing, barely consuming fuel, but constituting the life of the thinking faculty. *The Unnamable* is its trace, sour at being disturbed and being compelled to find something to be *of*, turner over of word after barely differentiated word, anxious only to be left in peace, unscrutinized. When you think to ask what you are thinking of, then, perhaps, you turn the harrowing spotlight on to The Unnamable.

He faces back to a past spent inventing the previous characters—"a ponderous chronicle of moribunds in their courses, moving, clashing, writhing or fallen in shortlived swoons"—and forward to a future in which "perhaps I shall be obliged, in order not to peter out, to invent another fairytale, yet another, with heads, trunks, arms, legs and all that follows, let loose in the changeless round of imperfect shadow and dubious light." He is represented, fraudulently, "up there in the world," by someone he first calls Basil, then decides to call Mahood. He has a future state, still more reduced, if he can succeed in getting it born, and this he calls Worm: "Worm the inexpugnable," the Undying Worm.

He starts to tell a story about Mahood, the one-legged man, which quickly, imperceptibly, turns into a story about himself, drawing on Mahood's testimony. He is moving, on his crutches, in an excruciating slow converging spiral with his numerous next-of-kin at its core, circling back from a world-wide sweep. They chatter, they comment, they restrain one another from distracting him with shouts of encouragement. "Often the cry went up, He's down! But in reality I had sunk to the ground of my own free will, in order to be rid of my crutches and have both hands available to minister to myself in peace and comfort. Admittedly it is difficult, for a man with but one leg, to sink to earth in the full force of the expression, particularly when he is weak in the head and the sole surviving leg flaccid for want of exercise, or from excess of it. The simplest thing then is to fling away the crutches and collapse. That is what I did." The old folk all die of ptomaine, while he tramples them without rancour. Is he there now, at that decaying centre? Is that where "here" is?

In the next Mahood story, Mahood is the man in the jar, armless and legless, across from a restaurant. The situation is elaborated in fantastic detail; the menu is affixed to the jar for passers-by to read, and the proprietress regards Mahood as "an undeniable asset." She has festooned his jar with Chinese lanterns to enhance its advertisement value. "Yes, I represent for her a tidy little capital and, if I should ever happen to die, I am convinced she would be genuinely annoyed. This should help me to live."

In fact Mahood (and again "I" and Mahood seem inextricable) is growing less embodied, rounder, more Platonic, rather like The Unnamable in whatever may be his present state. The narrative, if that is what it is, begins to teeter about the fulcrum of the Cartesian "ergo." I think, that is (alas) plain. Descartes went on smartly, "therefore I am." But am I, can I even come into existence? For ten pages we follow the effort of Worm to get born, an imperfectly satisfactory event. After a descant on being made of words (anyone in a book is made of words), a new surrogate emerges, simply "I," acquiring as it struggles into being the requisite accessories:

> There I am in any case equipped with eyes, which I open and shut, two, perhaps blue, knowing it avails nothing, for I have a head now too, where all manner of things are known, can it be of me I'm speaking, is it possible, of course not, that's another thing I know, I'll speak of me when I speak no more.

This "I" requires a name but does not receive one; panic is mounting; sentences grow longer and longer; the need is to be formed and defined and named, the anticipation is always of rebirth, the horror is when the birth occurs. Now Mahood is well in the past, as is apparently Worm; now the compulsion itself to narrate, narrate grows clearer, more insistent. "Yes, in my life, since we must call it so, there were three things, the inability to speak, the inability to be silent, and solitude, that's what I've had to make the best of." He proposes some words on the silence. And a terminal five-page sentence ends with the possibility that the end is yet one more beginning:

> Perhaps they [the words] have carried me to the threshold of my story, before the door that opens on my story, that would surprise me, if it opens, it will be I, it will be the silence, where I am, I don't know, I'll never know, in the silence you don't know, you must go on, I can't go on, I'll go on.

A difficult book, a Zero book? Certainly the book that, of all the fictions we have in the world, most cruelly reduces the scope of incident, the wealth of character. The utmost austerity has never dreamed of going so far. "I have lost my stick," wrote the dying Malone, "That is the outstanding event of the day," aware, Malone, that he is committing to paper a humour of disproportion; aware that in properly conducted works of fiction, such as he is not essaying, outstanding events are of ampler magnitude. He is having his little joke. But, "Air, the air," writes The Unnamable, "is there anything to be squeezed from that old chestnut?" and we have what very nearly qualifies, in this book, as an event, the wit that transforms "old chestnut" from a figure of speech into something squeezable (but spiky), performing a scrutable *deed*, but without humour, without pleasure. He is squeezing old chestnuts, worrying old dead themes, with heroic pertinacity, and with no such wink as Malone's, no pleasure such as Malone's in contemplating the Homeric splendours to which his incidents do not measure up. No, weary persistence, like the low vitality of the heart that beats during surgery, is setting sentence after sentence with unwavering punctilio, and it is with a bitter rictus that he contemplates the possibility of things getting livelier ("one never knows, does one, no"). "Perhaps Mahood will emerge from his urn and make his way towards Montmartre, on his belly, singing, I come, I come, my heart's delight." Small likelihood! And what a bitter effort it took to imagine even so much, even for a sentence's span.

For the theme of the book is heroism without drama: the heroism of the man undergoing torture, by nothing as dramatic as a Gestapo but by *accidie*, and having no recourse to Seconal or lewd imaginings. Flaubert envisioned a book which should be about Nothing, a book with no content, held together by the sheer style; but Nothing came rather easily to Flaubert, and as for style, he knew how to work for it. It would even have been, such a book, a self-indulgence. *The Unnamable* is far from self-indulgent, if only because the calm excellence of the writing shows no trace of narcissism; he accords himself no such pleasure.

"The sun shone, having no alternative, upon the nothing new." That is the first sentence of *Murphy*, and it invokes Nothing, and it is rather well pleased with itself. But the marvellous precisions of *The Unnamable* own no such taint. "I, of whom I know nothing, I know my eyes are open, because of the tears that pour from them unceasingly." No self-appreciation enhaloes the three I's, not even though the second is discriminated from the first and third in a manner to afford a philosopher *frisson*. "I know I am seated, my hands on my knees, because of the pressure against my rump, against the soles of my feet, against the palms of my hands, against my knees." This exhausts the list of pressures, and does so with finesse, but the finesse neither baits the reader as do the lists in *Watt*, nor expresses its own difficulty as do some of the enumerations in *Molloy*. "Against my palms the pressure is of my knees, against my knees of my palms, but what is it that presses against my rump, against the soles of my feet? I don't know. My spine is not supported." This exhausts the analysis of pressures. "I mention these details to make sure I am not lying on my back, my legs raised and bent, my eyes closed. It is well to establish the position of the body at the outset, before passing on to more important matters." This is grimly humorous, positing a maxim for which it is difficult to think of another application. Can this be said to be a maxim, if it has not some breadth of applicability? Yet it has the air of a maxim. Such penumbrae of logic, not dwelt on, are The Unnamable's little pleasures. But he never wavers in formulating, one by one, those beautifully shaped and balanced sentences, of perfect local clearness. Nor does he panic when uncertainty, or consternation, prolongs the sentences, accumulating phrases set off by commas.

Is the declarative sentence perhaps man's highest achievement? It may well be. No brute frames one. The uncivilized do no more than merely *name*, remaining at the mercy of the namable, or express by grunts and roars their pleasures and pains. The declarative sentence, then, which detaches from the big blooming buzzing confusion this thing, this subject, *this*, suavely validated by centuries of agreement and by dictionaries, and predicates with the aid of that mysterious agent the verb, to answer human desire, human satisfaction, creating a molecule of thought, a microcosm: in an absence of blooming and buzzing it can remain man's stay, excerpting, predicating. And always quoting; for all the words are old words, and all the phrases; it is something, if you are as horribly alone as The Unnamable, to know that comfort, "Ah, yes," he says, "I am truly bathed in tears," recognizing like an old friend a familiar expression, never till now of literal applicability. ("For I feel my tears coursing over my chest, my sides, and all down my back.") That is truly what it is to be bathed in tears; it is like Macmann gaining some insight into the expression, two is company. Language is this man's bitter company, grinding at his wordy-gurdy, in a book about Nothing that does not lose its power to fascinate, because the Nothing is being combatted by a moral quality: by the minimal courage that utters, utters, utters, without moan, without solecism.

Beckett and the End of Literature

Leo Bersani

Pour un nouveau roman: the very title for Robbe-Grillet's essays suggests a promotional aim which the essays themselves both realize and explain. Robbe-Grillet's decision to make explicit (even to simplify) his artistic goals in the frequently polemical formulas of his theoretical writing can be justified by the nature of the goals themselves. For the "New Novel," as Robbe-Grillet envisages it, will be nothing less than a model for human freedom; and if the model appears obscure or impenetrable, the novelist himself, it could be argued, has the duty of providing a kind of explanatory guide to help us to use his work—ultimately, to dismiss it—in the general enterprise of improvising a perhaps unprecedentedly free humanity.

Thus Robbe-Grillet, in *Pour un nouveau roman*, proselytizes for modern fiction as it has been practiced from Proust and Joyce to Beckett and Pinget in the hope that our "conversion" to modern art will coincide with radical transformations of the self and the world. In restating, often in oversimplified fashion, long-acknowledged achievements of the most interesting twentieth-century writers, Robbe-Grillet seems inspired by an urgently felt need to make those achievements available to the largest possible audience. From a man whose own work has been intelligently and generously praised, almost from the beginning, by such critics as Barthes, Blanchot, and Bernard Pingaud, Robbe-Grillet's complaints of all the hostile misunderstandings he has come up against may at first strike us as the sign of a petulant, insatiable appetite for praise. But we can also think of Robbe-Grillet's pursuit of popularity as proceeding from his conviction that unless art is popular and reaches minds less adventurous than those of Barthes and Blanchot, it can hardly be said

From *Balzac to Beckett: Center and Circumference in French Fiction.* © 1970 by Leo Bersani. Oxford University Press, 1970.

to contribute to that revolution in consciousness which it is Robbe-Grillet's most ambitious desire to promote. The popularizer is the revolutionary. If Robbe-Grillet's program for fiction does an injustice to the richness of his own fiction, it may at least expand the audience ready to confront that ambiguous richness. The novelist turned filmmaker has found an even more effective way of making himself felt outside literary circles. *L'Année dernière à Marienbad* is as interesting a performance of Robbe-Grillet's profound intentions as any of his novels. And not only do films reach a public far larger than the audience of *Pour un nouveau roman; Marienbad* never trumpets forth any of those tendentious summaries of literary history which, however necessary they may be in a program of literary proselytization, may make some of us inclined to come back to Robbe-Grillet's novels in a mood of distrust rather than in the disposition to recognize the novelist's freedom and to exercise our own.

Compared to Beckett, the Robbe-Grillet of *Pour un nouveau roman* is the innocent child of a new Enlightenment — one as naïvely confident and enthusiastic about human freedom as the old. Far from proselytizing for new novels or new men, Beckett has been austerely reticent about both his own intentions and his views on the art of the future. The nearest thing we have to an explicit statement of esthetic tastes or program is the cryptic, self-mocking *Three Dialogues* with Georges Duthuit, written and published for the first time in 1949 in *Transition*, toward the end of that period of extraordinary production (of about three years) when Beckett wrote the trilogy and *En attendant Godot*. The essay on Proust (1931) is a longer critical discussion, but it is much less useful than the ten pages or so of the Duthuit dialogues for an understanding of what Beckett has been trying to do (or trying not to do) in his most interesting work.

Like Robbe-Grillet, Beckett has an image of what art might become. Neither Masson nor Tal Coat lives up to what B. calls, in the dialogue on Masson, "my dream of an art unresentful of its insuperable indigence and too proud for the farce of giving and receiving." Since B. "exits weeping" when D. asks if we must really deplore the fact that Masson's painting admits " 'the things and creatures of Spring' . . . in order that what is tolerable and radiant in the world may continue," we must wait for the third dialogue, on Bram van Velde, for an elaboration of B.'s ideal of indigent art. When D. asks if Bram van Velde's painting is inexpressive, B. waits a fortnight before answering yes. Having in this way either established the importance (or perhaps the silliness) of the question, or raised doubts about using Bram van Velde to illustrate his idea, or suggested that to formulate the idea is an agony, perhaps an impossibility, B. finally suggests an alternative to "the common anxiety to express as much as possible, or as truly as possible, or as finely as possible, to the best of one's ability." Bram van Velde is the first in whose painting that anxiety—common to all those "whom we call great artists"—is absent. His work is "bereft, rid if you prefer, of occasion in every shape and form, ideal as well as material." And at last, at the end of this intriguing blend of humor, pathos, and eloquent verbal obscurity, B. gives us something like a key—or at least the right lock to work on—for his dream of art when he praises Bram van Velde as "the first to submit wholly to the incoercible absence of relation, in the absence of terms or, if you like, in the presence of unavoidable terms, the first to admit that to be an artist is to fail, as no other dare fail, that failure is his world and the shrink from it desertion, art and craft, good housekeeping, living."

The similarity between Robbe-Grillet and Beckett consists in little more than a rejection of certain traditional assumptions about the relation of art to the rest of life. And the rejection is such a widespread modern phenomenon that it hardly defines a particular affinity of talent or interest between these two writers. The common enemy (in theory, at least) is an esthetic of realistic reference: for both Robbe-Grillet and Beckett, the work of art is not dependent on, does not express anything that precedes it. It is against the notion of art's *derivation* from life that Robbe-Grillet argues when he writes that "the duration of the modern work is in no way a summary, a condensation of a more extended and more 'real' duration which would be that of the anecdote, of the story being told." The work of art constitutes its own reality, and for Robbe-Grillet this is equivalent to saying that it helps to constitute, to create reality itself. "The common anxiety to express"—which Beckett allows Bram van Velde to have the extraordinary privilege of abruptly ending in the history of modern art—can exist only as long as artists believe there are prior "occasions" to be expressed. Early nineteenth-century French society is the "material" occasion which Balzac aims to transpose, "as truly as possible," in *La Comédie humaine*. Proustian "essences" and Flaubert's "nature telle qu'elle est" could be thought of as the "ideal" occasions which *A la recherche* and *Madame Bovary* seek to make visible in language. If, Beckett seems to be saying, we could realize "the absence of terms," admit the impossibility of relating art *to* something else, we might finally have an art expressive of nothing but the resources it discovers in its own poverty-stricken, autonomous existence.

But the elusive complexities of Beckett's position become evident as soon as we examine how he connects the refusal of expressiveness in art to the praise of failure in art. For Robbe-Grillet, the dismissal of "real events" which art would merely summarize and condense is an immensely optimistic act of faith in art's ability to shape realities constrained, ideally, by nothing more than the number of combinations available to the imagination at its moments of greatest leisure. Robbe-Grillet's argument with the old ways of defining the artist's activity is based on a premise which, at least superficially, could hardly be thought of as disturbing: the work of art creates *more life*. A good deal of what might trouble us in the New Novel disappears once we realize, first, that the artist is not trying to separate himself from life, and, even more, that he wants to help us to be free men. There are no such "healthily" reassuring aspects in Beckett's thought. "Living," like "desertion, art and craft, good housekeeping," has nothing to do with being an artist. And in its independence from life, art creates *nothing at all*. For the artist Beckett has in mind, unlike Tal Coat and Matisse (who only disturb "a certain order on the plane of the feasible"), "there is nothing to express, nothing with which to express, nothing from which to express, no power to express, no desire to express, together with the obligation to express."

The dependence of Beckett's advocacy of failure on the opposition between expressive and inexpressive art is what I find most troubling in the *Dialogues*. The opposition itself suggests a hidden agreement with that view of art's derivative nature which, as I said a moment ago, Beckett seems to be rejecting as firmly as Robbe-Grillet. The assertion that expression is impossible is not the basis of a new definition of art; rather, it merely restates an old definition pessimistically. Since nothing is opposed to expression but the *absence* of expression, we may suspect that Beckett, instead of imagining some sort of authentic independence for art, has merely experienced the anguishing impossibility of deriving art from life and, as a result, has concluded that art can only be failure.

I do not mean the "merely" as a dismissal of this experience in Beckett, since his "fidelity to failure" has produced what I take to be the most impressive fiction in the West since Faulkner. But the *Dialogues* suggest something which I will develop in my discussion of Beckett's novels, and which provides us with a basis for some badly needed distinctions in our discussions of modern art. Beckett is disturbing without, in a sense, being radical; Robbe-Grillet, for all his reassuring rhetoric about freedom, is proposing the use of art for a revolution in human psychology. The *Dialogues*, even taken alone, suggest how alien such ambitions are to Beckett's temperament. Whereas Robbe-Grillet, in discarding an esthetic of expressiveness, attempts to find a new way to formulate what the artist does, Beckett seems to see being *in*expressive as the only alternative to the expressive. And yet how can we know that the artist is being inexpressive if he doesn't try — however reluctantly — to express? Indeed, B. insists that Bram van Velde cannot paint, but he is obliged to, and when D. asks why, B. must answer, "I don't know." Why this peculiar "obligation to express" when there is nothing to express and no desire or power to express? Even more fundamentally, what makes expression impossible?

The logic of failure is the subject of Beckett's work, but the "argument" would be uninteresting — for his readers, at any rate — if the will to fail, to say nothing, did not meet so many resistances. Beckett's predicament has been the opposite of Robbe-Grillet's. The open-ended novel, ready to receive a rich variety of unpredictable extensions both from the author and his public, tends, as we have seen, to be narrowed into the predictable, excessively determined structures of pathological compulsions in Robbe-Grillet's work. Beckett's struggle toward unrelieved monotony and total inexpressiveness, on the other hand, has taken on a kind of bizarre heroism given his fantastic talent for stylistic and dramatic diversity. Robert Garis has rightly emphasized the foolishness of complaints, from hostile critics, that Beckett simply "repeats himself" in each new work. Certainly, there is a kind of artistic variety, of which Picasso is the most spectacular modern example, which is simply alien to Beckett. But in the history of art, such variety is the exception rather than the rule, and Beckett's detractors are probably not bothered by what is at least an equally transparent "repetitiveness" in, say, Vermeer or Racine. As in Racine's tragedies from *Andromaque* through *Phèdre*, or, to choose a contemporary example, in Antonioni's films from *L'Avventura* to *Blow-up*, Beckett's work tries out various representations of what are readily recognizable as the persistent themes of Beckett's imagination. But in how many writers do such "fundamental notes" (to use Proust's expression) *not* exist, and could it not be argued that, except for Shakespeare and perhaps Picasso, a certain kind of "variety-without-identity" in art is the sign of an imagination which has never sounded its own most intense, and intensely particularizing interests? We have said almost nothing when we say that certain themes recur throughout an artist's work. Appreciation and criticism begin only when we discuss the quality of their treatment and the ways in which an artist exploits particular occasions in his art either for the reduction of his work to its most limited obsession (or inspiration), or for the expansion of the work to the point where it entertains more possibilities than its mere theme would, superficially, seem capable of accommodating.

Beckett's theatre offers the most striking proof of his ability to undermine a potentially monotonous vision of human desolation by dramatic images so richly differentiated that they defy any attempt to settle on a single definition of the vision. Estragon and Vladimir, for example, are touchingly tender, simple, and bungling clowns compared to the more sophisticated frantically self-centered, and continuously bitter Hamm and Clov. The central relationship in *En attendant Godot* includes a moving if irritated tenderness, and Didi and Gogo play together — with words and with things — like a couple of shabby burlesque-house comedians resigned to the poverty of their material and the obligation to go on. Hamm's appeals to Clov's sentiments in *Fin de partie* are, in comparison to Didi and Gogo's conjugal tolerance of each other, an unsettlingly potent blend of cynicism, sadistic taunting, and uncontrolled panic at the prospect of not being attended to. A series of highly diversified attachments characterize Beckett's theatrical couples. The naggingly protective way in which Vladimir takes care of Estragon is far from the sulky servitude that ties Clov to Hamm, or from the ambiguous need and gallantry with which Willie approaches Winnie at the end of *Happy Days*. And in *La Dernière bande*, the couple becomes the Krapp we see on the stage and the Krapp from the past whom we hear on the tape; what might have been an autobiographical monologue is a brilliantly executed confrontation between a passive Krapp on tape and the puzzled, curious, ironic Krapp of the present.

Furthermore, from the kind of grammatical exercise in suicidal longing which opens *Fin de partie* ("Fini, c'est fini, ça va finir, ça va peut-être finir") to Winnie's distinguished exclamation of joy at the beginning of *Happy Days* ("Another heavenly day"), Beckett has made an extraordinary leap from an almost unrelieved curse on life to an overwhelmingly touching image of dignified if desperate optimism. On the one hand, Estragon and Vladimir, and even Clov and Hamm, enjoy (so to speak) some freedom of movement compared to the near buried Winnie. But physical imprisonment and the possibility of suffocation in *Happy Days* are brilliantly set against all the reasons Winnie finds, in her startlingly inventive optimism, not to complain. The Beckett motifs do not disappear: everywhere in his work we find imprisonment, the horror of life, the wish for death or at least total and silent immobility, a crippled sense of time, and an exasperation with both the appearances of meaning in language and the problematic relations of thought and language to both significance and reality. But, given the diversified embodiments of these themes, any underlying structure of self we might define in his work would be no more than a mere skeleton of general attitudes. Not only do we have this variety of dramatic images; each work also emphasizes different aspects of the fundamental concerns. The theme of an inconceivable past, for example, takes various forms: Estragon's funny puzzlement about what happened yesterday in act 2 of *Godot*, and, in *Fin de partie*, the ash-can romanticism of Nagg and Nell's evocation of their engagement at Lake Como. References to what we are seeing as a play which the characters somehow feel obliged to accept the agony of participating in are more frequent in *Fin de partie* than elsewhere in Beckett's theatre, and the truth of the story Hamm tells from his past is put into doubt by his frequent shifting from a "narrative tone" to a "normal tone" in order to judge the quality and effectiveness of his performance.

Psychological diversity, changes of emphasis and tone, unfailingly original and surprising images of entrapment—and, of course, the astounding stylistic virtuosity of Beckett. The shift, for example, from a condensed, epigrammatic style (the vicious metaphysical punches at life) to the somber eloquence of Clov's last speeches or Hamm's "narrative tone" when he tells his story constitutes a range of expression impressively different from Estragon and Vladimir's "duets" and their more sustained colloquial speech. A comparable range can be found even in single passages. Lucky's famous exercise in "thinking" in *Godot* is certainly the most sense-devastating monologue in theatrical history. A basic structure of philosophical argumentation gives to the speech a mock coherence. Nonsense rhymes, mechanical repetitions, fractured syntax, the digressions and unexpected transitions within a more than three-page single sentence continuously threaten a fragile but stubbornly asserted order of thought with total chaos and unintelligibility. Despair about man and God is juxtaposed with the meaningless *quaquaquaqua* and the farcical references to scholarly investigations by Testew and Cunard (investigations "crowned by the Acacacacademy of Anthropopopometry of Essy-in-Possy"), and yet we somehow do move toward the almost buried, anticlimactic conclusion that man "wastes and pines" and is "fading" "in spite of the strides of physical culture the practice of sports such as tennis football running cycling swimming flying gloating riding gliding conating camogie skating tennis of all kinds dying flying sports of all sorts autumn summer winter winter tennis of all kinds hockey of all sorts penicilline and succedanea." Lucky's complicated and significantly insignificant chatter parodies the resources of language and of logic with a power that makes Ionesco's demonstrations of the absurd flexibility of words and logical structures in *La Cantatrice chauve* seem like facile if clever horseplay. Finally, would it be possible to confuse the styles of Molloy, Malone, and the Unnamable? The sardonic density of Molloy's speech, Malone's tired eloquence, and the Unnamable's breathless accumulation of brief, meaningless phrases within often monstrously long sentences make for a linguistic diversity which both parallels and mocks the movement toward total meaninglessness and impoverishment which gives to the trilogy its obvious unity.

That movement is, of course, the principal action of the trilogy; *Molloy, Malone meurt*, and *L'Innommable* record the most stupefying enterprise of mutilation in contemporary literature. In Balzac, Stendhal, Proust, and Robbe-Grillet, we have seen what might be called the "normal" or at least traditional relation between self-repetitions and self-diversification in fiction. In all these writers, and in spite of the important differences among them, the novel seems to be a testing-ground for uncovering and at the same time devising some means of escape from the self's most limiting (if fundamental) formulations of experience. In Beckett, this centrifugal aspiration is reversed, and in place of an effort to diffuse the self so that its liberty will not be crippled by a center of easily recognizable pressures and designs, we have an attempt to block all inventiveness and freedom and to return to the most extreme monotony of being. Now this experiment would have little dramatic interest if it were not for the almost incredible inventiveness I have just been discussing. The principal tensions of Beckett's work are generated by a strange, even ludicrous struggle against an imagination too rich to be successfully drugged into the uninteresting and meaningless monotony which it bizarrely yearns for. The trilogy gives us different forms of that struggle, and it concludes with the Unnamable's happy and unhappy failure to succeed in failing. What are the images and the logic of this exemplary experiment in self-stultification and in the stultification of literature?

L'Innommable is the most difficult work in the trilogy, but, novelistically, it is also the most impoverished. The philosophical issues implicit in the early sections of the trilogy become progressively more explicit, at the same time that the situations which embody them grow barer and barer. Beckett seems finally to make a desperate (and, as we shall see, impossible) effort to resolve certain questions without mediating them through dramatic imagery—as if the subject of his fiction existed in some pure version with which the fiction constantly interferes. *Molloy*, for all its peculiarity, has vestiges of a traditional novel with plot and character. Moran, who tells his story in the second half of the book, has more realistic attributes than any other figure in the trilogy. He has a house, a maid, and a son; he works as an agent for some secret society about which he himself knows very little; he is instructed at the beginning of the section to leave home and search for Molloy. This is the closest Beckett comes in the trilogy to a conventional richness of anecdote. But any conventional sort of interest we might take in the anecdote is dissolved from the very start. The mystery story is made absurd by an excess of mystery (Moran is told nothing at all about Molloy), and Moran's feeble attempts to formulate and carry out some lucid plan of action—and thereby to construct a tightly knit mystery story—are defeated by his brooding about the identity of Molloy, his nightmarish journey, and his gradual transformation into the crippled Molloy we already know from the first part of the novel.

But the Moran story does have suspense, comedy (especially in Moran's acidly witty account of how he is bringing up his dimwitted son), and pathos; and Moran has the most active project of any character in the trilogy. What the Beckett characters *have to do* becomes more and more meager. Molloy simply wants to visit his mother; Malone is just waiting to die; and the Unnamable's only wish and effort is to stop talking. Although Beckett is hardly trying to make the Moran adventure into a realistically serious detective story, there is more novelistic *matter* here than anywhere else. And Moran takes longer than any of the other narrator-protagonists to transform plot and character into nightmarishly comic fantasy and to invite the reader's disbelief and disinterest by making what he says as unbelievable, as confusing, and as insignificant as possible.

Molloy could be thought of as a crippled Moran, a Moran who has lost all illusions about being methodical and efficient, and who can tell us on the first page of his story: "The truth is I haven't much will left." (Although the Moran section obviously belongs, in the movement I'm speaking of, before the chronicle of Molloy, our acquaintance with Molloy adds an element of sinister recognition and presentiment to our reading of Moran's account of his gradual physical and moral paralysis.) Molloy is probably the most "appealing" of Beckett's characters. As an intermediate stage in the progression (or regression) from an active, self-confident Moran to the bedridden Malone and to the armless, legless thing planted in a jar in *L'Innommable*, the still mobile Molloy has a recognizable humanness and a range of adventure and response which the Unnamable would treat with impatient scorn. Molloy is continuously interesting and unpredictable. He is the occasion for Beckett's most impressive novelistic display of talents the trilogy will relentlessly work to destroy: a brilliantly comic use of colloquial speech, an extraordinary ability to create suspense over events or questions as trivial as possible, the knack of making humorous an uncompromising sourness and crankiness, and a gift for casual, persistent, and astonishingly inventive obscenity.

But the poverty of Molloy's projects and resources creates a dramatic vacuum in which he can develop the logic of a more radical poverty and thus prefigure his later incarnations in the trilogy. The crippled derelict is an ideal image for a philosophical apprenticeship. In his remarkable book on Beckett, Hugh Kenner has said that the trilogy carries the Cartesian process backwards, starting with a bodily *je suis* and ending with a pure cogito. In *Molloy*, the physical world is being prepared for that alien and autonomous cogito. Molloy's infirmities give him more time for reflection. Unable to move and to think at the same time, Molloy can enjoy, or suffer, an absolute mental concentration during the pauses between his painful movements. Even his lack of memory is an aid to pure thought: his incapacity to remember his mother's name or the name of the town she lives in diminishes the possibility of any effective action which might divert him from pursuing speculations to their useless or pseudo-conclusions. The difficulty of translating thought into action—of actually finding his mother, or simply of making his body obey his will—gives Molloy an opportunity to wander and get lost in the universe of words and ideas. Precisely because he has to face such elementary problems of locomotion, for example, the enigma of how immaterial thought can produce changes in the material world (an enigma raised by Descartes's dualism between mind and matter and to which Malebranche proposed the rather desperate solution of a Providential intervention for every physical event) becomes a dramatically concrete issue for Molloy. His thought rarely "reaches" matter, and this provides a grotesquely comic confirmation of that autonomy of mind which Descartes experienced as the strength and dignity of mind.

Beckett had already satirized the Cartesian optimism about ratiocination in *Watt*. Watt's futile probing into the "fixity of mystery" at Mr. Knott's house, and especially his breaking down of problems into interminable combinations and solutions, burlesque the easy confidence in analytic separations expressed in Descartes's second law for the infallible pursuit of truth: "divide each of the difficulties that I would be examining into as many elements as possible and as might be necessary to solve the difficulties more effectively." But Watt pursues these analytic proliferations with dogged seriousness, whereas Molloy engages in rational investigation with sarcastic thrusts at the process itself. Thought is mocked not just by the nature of the problems it attaches itself to (could Molloy's great love—Edith or Ruth?—have been really a man? how can he arrange his sixteen stones in his four pockets so that he won't suck any of them twice before sucking all the others?), but also by Molloy's comments about his own thinking. The diarrhetic flow of Molloy's prose includes a kind of parenthetical irony absent from *Watt*. The essentially aimless and unconvinced nature of his chatter is emphasized by all the sentences beginning with "And" (as if words could do nothing but accumulate), and, most effectively, by his casual but sharp sarcasm. Molloy handles words he happens to say like some comically disgusting foreign matter he watches passing through his mind. From a window in Lousse's house, Molloy sees a full moon; but he thinks he remembers that just "the night before, or the night before that, yes, more likely," the moon had been a mere "shaving," and that a little while after its appearance to him, he had decided to visit his mother.

And if I failed to mention this detail in its proper place, it is because you cannot mention everything in its proper place, you must choose, between the things not worth mentioning and those even less so. For if you set out to mention everything you would never be done, and that's what counts, to be done, to have done. Oh I know, even when you mention only a few of the things there are, you do not get done either, I know, I know. But it's a change of muck. And if all muck is the same muck that doesn't matter, it's good to have a change of muck, to move from one heap to another a little further on, from time to time, fluttering you might say, like a butterfly, as if you were ephemeral. And if you are wrong, and you are wrong, I mean when you record circumstances better left unspoken, and leave unspoken others, rightly, if you like, but how shall I say, for no good reason, yes, rightly, but for no good reason, as for example that new moon, it is often in good faith, excellent faith.

This distance which Molloy mockingly keeps from his own speech raises the possibility of a Molloy distinct from his speech. First of all, what connection is there between the account of Molloy's adventures which we are reading and those adventures as they really happened? Molloy warns us that the "limpid language" he now uses expresses nothing more than his

merely complying with the convention that demands that you either lie or hold your peace. For what really happened was quite different. And I did not say, Yet a little while, at the rate things are going, etc., but that resembled perhaps what I would have said, if I had been able. In reality I said nothing at all, but I heard a murmur, something gone wrong with the silence [quelque chose de changé dans le silence] and I pricked up my ears, like an animal I imagine, which gives a start and pretends to be dead. And then sometimes there arose within me, confusedly, a kind of consciousness, which I express by saying, I said, etc., or, Don't do it Molloy, or, Is that your mother's name? said the sergeant, I quote from memory.

What "kind of consciousness," exactly? The trilogy and *Comment c'est* are Beckett's efforts to approach that reality of consciousness about which language lies, to torture words out of their "limpidity" and significance so that they may let us hear just "how it was" in the silence. The furiously conscientious chroniclers who are Beckett's narrators all insist that they live "far from words," as Molloy says. Ignorant of "the meaning of being," Molloy can only walk among the "ruins" of his self, "a place with neither plans nor bounds and of which I understand nothing, not even of what it is made, still less into what. And the thing in ruins. I don't know what it is, what is was, nor whether it is not less a question of ruins than the indestructible chaos of timeless things, if that is the right expression."

Molloy tells the stories he doesn't believe in and uses a language which doesn't express anything with comparative nonchalance. Anxious only to "finish dying," he nonetheless accepts, with docile if ironic obedience, the mysterious punishment of having to write about a past made of silence and an inexpressible self. Furthermore, he has just enough purposeful behavior, and just enough mobility, to be mainly preoccupied with telling a story; compared with *Malone meurt* and *L'Innommable*, *Molloy* is an action-packed narrative. "And truly it little matters," Molloy claims, "what I say, this, this or that or any other thing," but that doesn't prevent him from telling a fairly stable story about himself and the way things happened. The doubts about the very possibility of telling a story will be more fully dramatized by protagonists who either don't remember or don't believe in their pasts, and who are therefore more "free" to consider the distance between what they say and what they are.

This mysterious distance—unlocatable, unbridgeable—becomes a more explicit obsession in *Malone meurt*. Malone has nothing to do but wait in bed for the death whose imminence he announces in the novel's first sentence: "I shall soon be quite dead at last in spite of all." ("Je serai quand même bientôt tout à fait mort enfin.") He is finally being "repaid" for having lived by being allowed to die. The only important thing now is to stay quiet, to "be natural at last," to "die tepid, without enthusiasm." Malone decides to pass the time telling stories, "calm" stories with "no ugliness or beauty or fever," stories "almost lifeless, like the teller." But the confusions and discouragements to come—which will of course make the interest of the book—are prefigured by Malone's excessive and already useless caution on the first pages. He recognizes several dangers which threaten to break his calm: the tendency to ask questions, the temptation to think ("If I start trying to think again I shall make a mess of my decease"), his uncertainty about the number of stories to tell, his wondering whether he should begin or end with the inventory of his possessions. No matter; with the sense of "making a great mistake," Malone nonetheless decides to divide his time into five ("into five what?"): "Present state, three stories, inventory, there" (with "an occasional interlude"). This mixture of fear, fussiness, weak self-assurance, and unconvincing good faith gives to the beginning of *Malone meurt* its highly original comic tension. Beckett has managed to announce an investigation into the reality and possibility of literary play entirely in terms of Malone's anxious efforts to settle calmly on the right schedule of his last days or weeks. Something is already pulling Malone away from his stories. "It is playtime now. I find it hard to get used to that idea. The old fog calls." Will Malone be able to play? And what is the "fog" which draws speech back into silence, which turns all stories—all literature—into ruins?

"I never knew how to play, until now," Malone writes at the beginning. He often tried, "but it was not long before I found myself alone, in the dark. That is why I gave up trying to play and took to myself for ever shapelessness and speechlessness, incurious wondering, darkness, long stumbling with outstretched arms, hiding. Such is the earnestness [le sérieux] from which, for nearly a century now, I have never been able to depart." Malone's disease of "earnestness" (a weak word to designate his yearning for nothingness) will return to plague him as he attempts to tell calm stories clearly. He stops in the middle of anecdotes out of boredom and disgust, he abruptly changes the names and lives of the characters he invents, and he moves back and forth between his stories and thoughts about himself. In a sense, his failure is Beckett's success. The richness of this part of the trilogy consists in its multiple but continuously suspended points of interest. Our expectations of drama are teased and disappointed by the incompleteness and triviality of the anecdotes; even the barest sense of psychological consistency is destroyed by Sapo's sudden transformation into Macmann; and the frequent returns to Malone in bed add to our reading of the stories he tells a suspenseful curiosity about how close the narrator is to death. It is therefore obviously not enough to say that *Malone meurt* is a novel which carries out its own destruction. Beckett, the plotter of that destruction, has weaved so many self-negating processes into a single narrative web that the very interferences among them create a complexity of drama and suspense which, for the reader, works against the pull toward fog, disappearance, total failure, and the silence of death. It is nonetheless true that for Malone the pleasure of dying is almost spoiled by his inability to keep out of the fog long enough for the night to come. What destroys the resolution of the early pages is Malone's inability to talk about anything but himself (to be able to do that would be "to play"), at the same time that his stories lose their "calm" by becoming mirrors for the agitated "fog" of his own being.

A curious vindication of storytelling takes place in *Malone meurt*. It is as if Beckett were trapped into an implicit recognition of the *possibility* of storytelling. *L'Innommable* could be imagined as a furious revenge against

Malone's demonstration of imagination as adequate to being. Malone begins with a half-hearted attempt to tell the story of the young Sapo, remarking that "nothing is less like me than this patient, reasonable child, struggling all alone for years to shed a little light upon himself, avid of the least gleam, a stranger to the joys of darkness." But Malone's storytelling will become both interesting and urgently necessary only when Sapo is transformed into Macmann, a character much closer to Malone himself. The account of Macmann's stay at the asylum at the end of the novel is one of Beckett's most extraordinary performances. The range of invention is staggering: from Moll and Macmann's hilariously disgusting love affair to Macmann's nightmarish hallucinations when he tries to escape from the asylum, and to the inmates' outing with the philanthropic Lady Pedal and Lemuel's casual slaughter of the sailors and Lady Pedal at the end.

Most important, this imaginative virtuosity spectacularly confirms the self-expressiveness of verbal play. For the wildness of the Macmann episode dramatizes the death agony of Malone. The obscene blasphemies, the confused perceptions, the murders, and the final vision of the inmates' "grey bodies" on the bay ("Silent, dim, perhaps clinging to one another, their heads buried in their cloaks, they lie together in a heap, in the night") trace Malone's last moments alive in bed. Sequestration and annihilation: the two main themes of Macmann's life at the asylum bring us back to the imprisoned Malone waiting for death. The identification is explicit in the last lines Malone writes. Lemuel "raises his hatchet" again, but "he will not hit anyone any more," and the hatchet becomes the stick and the pencil with which Malone will never touch anything any more. Lemuel's murderous violence suggests the drunken suicidal elation of Malone's last moments, and the connections between hatchet, stick, and pencil define this *premortem* literature as the symbolic murder of symbolic selves. To tell stories is to draw things into the self, as Malone uses his stick to draw things close to his bed. For Malone, it is also the ambiguous act of creating and destroying figures who are never exactly the self but who represent it sufficiently to become the objects of self-destroying impulses. Unwilling to talk about himself and unable not to, having opposed the play of telling stories to the fog of being, Malone ends with an anecdote which embodies his profound antipathy to anecdote at the same time that it appears to give shape and speech to the shapeless and speechless fog.

Behind the intermittent eloquence of Malone's style lies a tolerance of language perhaps made possible by his certainty that he will soon die. "There is no use indicting words, they are no shoddier than what they peddle [Ils ne sont pas plus creux que ce qu'ils charrient]." The successful act of expression which is Macmann's story depends on a double failure: the inability to play calmly with stories alien to the self, and the failure to drop the story for the sake of a return to "the rapture of vertigo, the letting go, the fall, the gulf, the relapse to darkness, to nothingness, to earnestness, to home." Confident of dying, Malone lets himself be seduced into expression. But if the richness of what he says gives the lie to the impossibility of expression, the mad and murderous universe evoked does locate the inspiration for Malone's most sustained story in a wish to mutilate and end what he invents. "Of myself I could never tell, any more than live or tell of others." However contested this proposition may be by the work in which it occurs, it is also somewhat confirmed by Malone's half-hearted effort to tell boring stories at the beginning of the novel, and by that promise of vertigo and finally annihilation (both for himself and for his characters) which seems to support Malone in the chronicle of Macmann. But *why* is Malone unable "to tell of himself" ("se raconter") and why, as a result, does he take up his pencil only to plot movements toward the moment when he will have to let it go?

The answer is suggested in the passage from which I have been quoting in the last paragraph. There Malone speaks — with an ambiguity made greater by the differences between the French and English texts — of someone else, or perhaps of two other "people." In his returns "home" — "to darkness, to nothingness" — he has been welcomed by someone "waiting for me always, who needed me and whom I needed, who took me in his arms and told me to stay with him always." What relation exists between Malone and this inhabitant of darkness? The next sentence in French is simply: "Voilà que je commence à m'exalter," while the English version teases us with: "There I am forgetting myself again." And is Malone still alluding to this mysterious figure when he goes on to evoke "another, far beneath me and whom I try to envy, of whose crass adventures [les plates aventures] I can now tell at last, I don't know how"? The suggestion of a self "beneath" the self is absent in French, where Malone says of this other presence only that he "ne me vaut pas" (and who may be just Malone projected into inaccurate stories). Finally, after writing that he has never been able to tell of himself or of others, Malone raises a possibility he hardly dares to believe in. "To show myself now, on the point of vanishing, at the same time as the stranger, and by the same grace, that would be no ordinary last straw." The "stranger" may be someone different from Malone, but he may also be a Malone deeper than Malone, "beneath" him, to whom he returns as to a familiar home after his useless attempts to tell of others and of a less essential self. "What an end,"

Malone ambiguously writes when he thinks of a simultaneous death for all these personae, or for the "real" self and its personae: "Then live, long enough to feel, behind my closed eyes, other eyes close."

It is of course difficult to say to whom these other eyes belong. Are they those of a self beyond (or prior to) all definition and expression, or of an impersonal presence which nonetheless inhabits the depths of personality, or perhaps of some jealous, uncreated divinity "who can neither live nor suffer the sight of others living"? *Malone meurt* provides no answers to these questions, but in the tensions it sets up between Malone's will to play and his inability to play, and between his contention that he cannot talk of himself or of others and the proof he offers of finding himself—and his death—through talking of others, this second work in the trilogy plunges us into that "impenetrable tangle of relationships between the essential Self and the apparent self" which Richard D. Coe defines as the "central theme of Beckett's philosophy." The distinctive feature of *L'Innommable* is that there is no "tangle" between the two, but only a continuously reiterated chasm. "I, say I. Unbelieving," mutters the Unnamable at the start of his anonymous monologue. "I seem to speak, it is not I, about me, it is not about me." *L'Innommable* is the Beckett protagonist's desperate attempt to stop talking, to "overcome . . . the fatal leaning toward expressiveness [surmonter . . . le funeste penchant à l'expression]," and to arrive at a silence different from the pauses between words, at "the real silence, . . . that of the drowned," where the self perhaps merely *is*, but where being seems equivalent to nonbeing.

Malone in bed deliberately transforms Sapo into Macmann. The Unnamable doesn't know where he is, but he has always been there ("my appearances elsewhere having been put in by other parties"). And among the various names and images in the narrative (Mahood and Worm; the gigantic creature unrolled around the earth, the thing planted in a jar near a city's slaughterhouses, the round ball that may "snowball" into a man), there are not metamorphoses but rather the aimless wandering of a voice which occasionally evokes a shape or a name but never associates the two long enough to establish an identity. Macmann and Sapo have consistent, almost realistic personalities compared to Mahood and Worm. The Unnamable even shifts from "he" to "I" in the middle of a description, or from "I" to "he." The designations of person and the distinction between singular and plural are the farces of an arbitrary grammar: "No sense in bickering about pronouns and other parts of blather. The subject doesn't matter, there is none." Other Beckett figures—Mercier and Camier, Murphy, Molloy, and Malone—seem to be circulating around the Unnamable, and the possibility that, like him, they have always been there retrospectively reduces Molloy's search for his mother and Malone's death to the Unnamable's fictions. The long voyage from Mercier and Camier to the Unnamable has been an effort to end all voyages, to be finally in a place one cannot go to: "The essential is never to arrive anywhere, never to be anywhere, neither where Mahood is, nor where Worm is, nor where I am, it little matters thanks to what dispensation."

In this process of "retrenchment," as Ruby Cohn has aptly called it, anecdote, character, movement, desire, and intelligence have been gradually reduced in the hope that they can at last be dispensed with completely. The Unnamable throws off all the personae which he claims, have been foisted on him by "masters" who want him to confuse himself with his roles. He wonders if now he will be able to express only himself, "to be a little as I always was and never could be." The setting of *L'Innommable* may be "the place where one finishes vanishing" ["l'endroit où l'on finit de se dissiper"], and the image of someone who is nothing more than a "big talking ball" expresses the anguished need of the Beckett hero to get rid of all the things that "stick out" ("tout ce qui dépasse est tombé," says the Unnamable), from some mysterious core of being—everything from bodily protuberances to fictional characters and stories and, finally, verbal inventiveness or expression itself.

The Unnamable thus "refers" us to a self with which we are not to confuse either his characters or even what he himself says. If we take the dream of this self seriously in Beckett, we should perhaps do no more than repeat that it is indeed unnamable, indescribable. But we can draw a circle around that invisible point by tracing the possible motivations and the consequences of the search itself. A writer's experience of the power and apparent expressiveness of language may lead him to an intuition of and an interest in a reality which language cannot express, from which language in fact isolates him. Novelistic invention could be thought of as self-dispersion rather than as self-expression, as a loss or waste of energy which writers may alternately refuse and consent to. The writer's answer to the optimism of Descartes's cogito might be imagined as: "I invent, therefore I am not." Beckett's novels dramatize this radical doubt about the relation between imaginative language and the self: where am I in the world I am creating? In spite of his call for an inexpressive, autonomous art, Beckett's work is perhaps motivated by a deeper fantasy of literature as the passive receptacle for a self entirely independent of literary inventiveness. For what the Unnamable hates in expression is that it is *not* expression, but, inevitably, invention. More exactly, every expression is an invention. It violates the purity of being with the accidents of personality, language, and time.

To be *anything* is not to be. The Beckett "ideal" seems to me more mysteriously abstract than the comparatively intelligible disappearance of the self into the universe which Molloy occasionally experiences. If the ultimate Beckett "home" contains the entire universe, it is only in the sense that the inhabitant of that home has not yet lost the possibility of being everything and everywhere by being born into a particular body and a particular place in the universe. The Beckett hero—the one we never see—is unborn. Beckett's difficult progress toward that realization can be measured by the difference between the still rather vague notion of a self merely "improved out of all knowledge" in *Murphy*, and the brilliantly simple device of making the Unnamable the victim of a conspiracy to force him just to live. His persecutors want him to be a man, to be born. They give him roles to play (which nicely accounts for the Beckett oeuvre), but he has resisted being identified with them (which dismisses the Beckett oeuvre). *L'Innommable* is Beckett's allusion to the absence behind his personae and the voices which speak through them. It is his most radical experiment—short of complete silence—in drawing his creation back into its uncreated source. An absurd, suicidal adventure, the very authenticity of which is undoubtedly guaranteed by Beckett's frank recognition that the inviolate, essential self "lives" only in the refusal to be, is equivalent to the death of the self.

Maurice Blanchot, whose *Thomas l'Obscur* records an analogous retreat, has called the Unnamable "a being without being . . . the empty place where the idleness of an empty speech talks, a place more or less successfully covered over by a porous and dying *I*." For Blanchot, that "place," which is the Beckett hero's "home," is also the "home" of literature: *L'Innommable* is "the pure approach to the moment from which all books come, to that original point where the work probably loses itself." Beckett's work thus moves toward a self without personality and a literature without books. It seems hardly necessary to say that the failure to reach such goals is what allows them to be pursued. The metaphysical pathos of Beckett's work is that it exists. It has, however, existed by tending more and more to destroy itself. The voice which speaks in *L'Innommable*, a voice "not listening to itself but to the silence that it breaks," moves toward a meaningless verbal flow in which the silence can perhaps be heard. But the Unnamable also knows that he will go on, that he has to go on, tortured by the distance between his words and "how it is," a distance which, incidentally, the resurgent structure and inventiveness of *Comment c'est* (1961) simply confirm as unbridgeable. Moran had already spoken of all language as an "écart de langage," which in English becomes "an excess of language." Language is always in excess of being, and the end (goal and disappearance) which is silence is perhaps best approximated by a stupefyingly excessive language, by the long sentences in the second half of *L'Innommable*, sentences filled with commas separating and isolating and equalizing inexhaustible verbal signs or gasps which finally reduce the story, the language, and the mind of the narrator to an insignificant, rambling murmur.

Now the Beckett protagonists constantly complain of being forced to write and to speak. Life and language are punishments—although life itself seems to be the crime, so that they are entrapped in a sadistically imposed penance which increases their guilt. All Beckett's commentators have responded to the anguished religious sensibility in his work. Beginning with the easy game of reading *Godot* in the light of the broad hint which the title gives us and which the play neither confirms nor denies, we can hardly miss the combination of angry, mocking blasphemy and need without hope which characterizes Beckett's Job-like relation to God and his mystified fascination with the Crucifixion. God comes into existence in Beckett's world very much as He comes to exist in Descartes's world. The Cartesian *cogito* is naturally analyzed in the *Discours de la méthode* as a process of rational deduction, but it appears to have been experienced as an intuition which simultaneously proves human existence and divine existence. The latter is contained in the certainty of the former, and one could condense the rational sequence of part 4 of the *Discours* into the equation: I doubt = God exists. The Beckett divinity is also contained in the existence of the Beckett protagonist, and the protagonist's existence is also confirmed by a kind of "doubt" or "thought." But the Cartesian intuition is of course parodied: "doubt" is hopeless misery, and, instead of a good and perfect God being guaranteed by the very imperfection of doubt from which man suffers, Beckett's characters invoke a sadistic demon also "guaranteed," but this time by the impenetrable enigma of man's continuing to live an unlivable life. "Imperfection," far from certifying a perfect God from Whom the notion of perfection must proceed, more convincingly implies a divinity whose malevolent existence is needed to explain an aberration as monstrous as life.

"I say it as I hear it," Bom reminds us over and over again in *Comment c'est*. Life and the novel are *dictated*. The Unnamable, whose only real speech would be silence, tells us that he has no voice but must speak, "that is all I know, it's round that I must revolve, of that I must speak, with this voice that is not mine, but can only be mine, since there is no one but me, or if there are others, to whom it might belong, they have never come near me, I won't delay just now to make this clear [ils ne viennent pas jusqu'à moi, je n'en dirai pas davantage, je ne serai pas plus clair]." And a few pages further on: "Having nothing to say, no words but the words of others, I have to speak." He *is*, literally, *nothing* but words: "I'm in words, made of words, others' words, what others." The impossibility of any speech adequate to being is dramatically rendered in *L'Innommable* by the physical impossibility of speech. In *Molloy* and *Malone meurt*, Beckett makes almost realistic provisions for the plausibility of his narrative by making Molloy, Moran, and Malone writers. But how can a round ball speak? How can an armless creature write? No attempt is made to answer these questions, just as no attempt is made to explain how the Beckett protagonist can complain of using the words of others when the complaint itself, has, presumably, to be made in the words of others.

These are perhaps mysteries of divine machination, but we could also formulate them in terms of the impossible relation Beckett has established between the writer and his creation. The voice forcing Molloy, Moran, Malone, and the Unnamable to speak is, of course, Beckett's voice. And he has brilliantly expressed the enigma of identity in fiction (where am I in the world I am creating?) by having his characters protest, for and against him, that their reality is not to be confused with his. All words are naturally the words of others, since others use the same language as we do, and since language itself obviously expresses or proceeds from no single human subject. To this general sense of the impersonality of language, Beckett adds the much more particular drama of alienation and hostility between himself and his fictional world. The Beckett heroes, by refusing to be identified with the imagination they must "carry" in their words, enact in reverse the writer's rebellion against being confused with the creatures of his imagination. The trilogy's protagonists are the vehicles not simply of language, but more especially of Beckett's language. Thus the words we read belong to someone outside the novel, but they tell the story of someone in the novel who claims that his story cannot be told. The impenetrable divinity is Beckett, who will only talk *about* Malone and the Unnamable; but Malone and the Unnamable will allow themselves to be made to talk about themselves only if they can duplicate, with respect to their own creations, their author's implicit disclaimer with respect to them.

A terror at being identified, a despair because identification is impossible: this is the profound motivation which subjects Beckett's extraordinary language to a violent rejection of language. Beckett and his characters will perhaps go on because, as they say, they have to go on, and they perhaps have to go on simply as an alternative to the ecstasy and horror of drawing in their lips, as Winnie says in *Happy Days*, and reaching the absolute expressiveness of nonexpression. But they have been going on less and less in recent years, and while it is both right and too easy to say that Beckett has already given us more than any other living writer, we must also take his suicidal literature seriously enough to be willing to define our own participation in its longings for annihilation.

Subjectivity as the Autogenous
Cancellation of Its Own Manifestations

Wolfgang Iser

The approach to the theme of subjectivity in Beckett's trilogy may be summed up by a remark of Nietzsche's, describing the workings of consciousness: "The interpretative character of all events. There is no such thing as an event in itself. What happens is a group of appearances, selected and brought together by an interpreting being. . . . There are no given facts. And it is the same with feelings and with ideas: in becoming conscious of them, I make a selection, a simplification, an attempt at forming a gestalt: that is what is meant by becoming conscious—a completely active re-formation." Beckett's trilogy makes the reader conscious of this process itself, revealing not only the effects of such a "reformation" but also the conditions that bring it about.

The very titles of the three novels—*Molloy, Malone Dies,* and *The Unnamable*—draw attention to the first-person narrator's withdrawal into anonymity. While in the third novel he is the unnamable, in the first two his names seem like mere disguises which he has assumed. In retrospect, the masks of the unnamable appear to indicate certain references, limitations, and attitudes which have lost their validity in the final novel. But the unnamable is not completely free of the names which he has borne and which now prevent him from being at peace in his anonymity. The first two novels have prepared the way for the third, but they continue to exercise their influence upon it.

Perhaps the most durable of these influences is the extraordinary style, which in *Molloy* is fully formed. The sentence construction in this and in the subsequent novels is frequently composed of direct contradictions. A statement is followed by the immediate retraction of what has been stated. The degree of contradiction varies from modification or patent undermining right through to total negation, as for instance at the very end of *Molloy*: "I shall learn. Then I went back into the house and wrote, It is midnight. The rain is beating on the windows. It was not midnight. It was not raining." This variable but ceaseless alternation between statement and negation remains the characteristic feature of the style in all three novels. The striking culmination of this trend at the close of *Molloy* is certainly not accidental, for it is a magnified echo of the crescendo and decrescendo of all the individual sentences. The technique results in a total devaluation of language by accentuating the arbitrariness with which it is applied to the objects it seeks to grasp.

The attentive reader will not be altogether unprepared for these closing sentences. Through the nature of his narrative, Molloy gives a number of indications, both direct and indirect, as to what conditions all these contradictory statements. He himself immediately questions a great number of his own findings—as, for instance, right at the beginning of the novel: "A and C I never saw again. But perhaps I shall see them again. But shall I be able to recognise them? And am I sure I never saw them again? And what do I mean by seeing and seeing again?"

These are questions posed by a consciously reflecting mind which seeks to uncover the presuppositions that condition a statement, and thus to show that that statement is a barely tenable version of the facts it attempts to convey. However, the first-person narrator can only formulate his observations of himself and his surroundings by making such statements, for they are the only means by which he can build up the reality he wants to describe. And so whatever conditions his perception, becomes incorporated in the conclusions he draws from that perception. The world thus constituted is comprehensible and describable—but the question is whether this is the world the narrator is actually trying to capture in his narrative.

Molloy is fully aware of this question:

> And when I say I said, etc., all I mean is that I knew confusedly things were so, without knowing exactly what it was all about. And every time I say, I said this, or, I said that, or speak of a voice saying, far away inside me, Molloy, and then a fine phrase more or less clear and simple, or find myself compelled to attribute to others intelligible words, or hear my own voice uttering to others more or less articulate sounds, I am merely complying with the convention that demands you either lie or hold your peace. For what really happened was quite different. And I did not say,

Yet a little while, at the rate things are going, etc. . . . In reality I said nothing at all, but I heard a murmur, something gone wrong with the silence, and I pricked up my ears, like an animal I imagine, which gives a start and pretends to be dead. And then sometimes there arose within me, confusedly, a kind of consciousness, which I express by saying, I said, etc., or, Don't do it Molloy, . . . Or which I express without sinking to the level of oratio recta, but by means of other figures quite as deceitful, as for example, It seemed to me that, etc., or, I had the impression that, etc., for it seemed to me nothing at all, and I had no impression of any kind.

This reflection is embedded in a process which Molloy would like to narrate but which he has to falsify because the convention of narration has its own laws, that have little or no bearing upon actual reality. Narration sets out to convey something which cannot possibly be conveyed by it, and so any narrative representation must inevitably be a lie. Molloy is fully aware that both the presentation and the communication of any given reality can only result in the alteration of that reality, for the facts will be set in one context or another, and so it will be the context and not the facts that will be communicated. On the other hand, reality only takes shape for the observer in accordance with his own presuppositions. The first-person narrator can only bring this knowledge to bear by offering the reality he has observed as the mere product of his mode of presentation, which is unlikely to coincide with whatever may be the true nature of that reality.

This insight is conveyed by the alternation of statement and modification throughout the narrative, for every statement imposes a particular order on things, thus excluding much of what they might really be. The conscious mind that conducts the operation of stating and retracting is aware of the incongruence between object and meaning, and this is why the perceptions recorded in Molloy's monologue are constantly accompanied by reflections on how they took place and what conditioned the manner in which they took place. Thus a single act of perception often releases a chain reaction of self-observation, as the narrator seeks to find out what brought about the act and why it took the form it did take. This process is sometimes taken so far that the original perception and the self-questionings that spring from it become completely dissociated.

This dissociation is conveyed by the self-cancelling structure of the sentences, which indicate that a world perceived only in terms of phenomena is just as much a product of the conscious mind as one that is deliberately given a specific form. As both perception and interpretation of phenomena are qualified equally as offshoots of the conscious mind, the reality perceived must in itself clearly be totally devoid of any meaning of its own. Thus the conscious mind turns its attention away from the interpretation of things and onto its own actual processes of interpretation.

The self-representation of Malone and of the unnamable takes place in the light of this knowledge. Malone lies in a room; he knows that he is soon going to die, only what concerns him is not death but the impossibility of getting to the end of himself. As the world around him gradually disintegrates, so his conscious mind becomes increasingly active, filling the void with various forms. Molloy had still had an overall view of his own fragmented story, but for Malone this degree of self-detachment has shrunk considerably. Molloy had realized that all presentation is "re-formation"—summed up by his pithy epigram "Saying is inventing"—and this realization is taken for granted during Malone's preoccupation with himself. Malone cannot therefore tell himself his own story before his death, because as a piece of self-representation this could only reflect its own conditional nature. And so he decides to tell himself stories which are quite obviously fictitious. Typically, he regards his intention of filling in the rest of his life with stories as "playing," diverting him from what would otherwise be the compulsion to write about himself—for whatever he were to maintain in writing about himself would only be how he appears to himself, but not what he actually is. He is therefore left with the choice of telling stories or, as sometimes happens, writing about writing. In the first case he knows he is dealing with fictions; in the second he knows he is dealing with the mode of fiction itself. In telling stories, Malone knows he is telling lies, but this releases him from the terrible curse of describing his own situation and therefore telling lies about himself. He does not want to be the object of his own observations, even though he is really concerned with the question of who he is. But in due course his fictitious stories begin to bore him, and he breaks off with the following:

> What tedium. And I call that playing. I wonder if I am not talk-
> ing yet again about myself. Shall I be incapable, to the end, of
> lying on any other subject? I feel the old dark gathering, the
> solitude preparing, by which I know myself, and the call of that
> ignorance which might be noble and is mere poltroonery. Already
> I forget what I have said. That is not how to play. . . . Perhaps
> I had better abandon this story and go on to the second, or even
> the third. . . . No, it would be the same thing. I must simply
> be on my guard, reflecting on what I have said before I go on

and stopping, each time disaster threatens, to look at myself as I am. That is just what I wanted to avoid.

He finds, then, that the stories are about himself after all, and the more stories he tries to tell, the clearer it becomes to him that the material is taken from his own life. "All the stories I've told myself, clinging to the putrid mucus, and swelling, swelling, saying, Got it at last, my legend." And together with this insight goes the knowledge that such stories are only pretexts to avoid having to get to grips with the real self:

> All is pretext, Sapo and the birds, Moll, the peasants, those who in the towns seek one another out and fly from one another, my doubts which do not interest me, my situation, my possessions, pretext for not coming to the point, the abandoning, the raising of the arms and going down, without further splash. . . . The horror-worn eyes linger abject on all they have beseeched so long, in a last prayer, the true prayer at last, the one that asks for nothing.

In his stories he may see his legend, but at the same time he knows that this legend—even though it has sprung entirely from his own ideas— cannot be identical with his real self. After all, he has always been conscious of the fact that such stories are nothing but fabrications, and so clearly the legend arising from the stories can at best only be a distorted reflection of a distorted reflection of himself.

Subjectivity in *Malone Dies* is presented in the form of a ceaseless dialectic that is never synthesized. If the last, true prayer is for nothing, this desire is an answer to the need for self-understanding. In praying for nothing, the self seeks to release itself from this need. And yet the very facts of life, the desolation of tedium, the openness of the situation, and the void of approaching death drive Malone to counteract the void, tedium and openness with something specific. That is why he tells his stories, though he immediately retracts any meaning that threatens to become specific. This paradoxical behavior is symptomatic of his situation, the implications of which are made clear by the idea of playing—which is what Malone calls his story-telling. The stories are "play" insofar as they are not devised for the sake of an ultimate meaning but only for meanings that will ward off the void. They provide a diversion and not a destination. In them, Malone continually goes beyond his known self in order to try and get to a last frontier of himself—a point which he is fully aware can never be reached.

Malone sees himself confronted by an unanswerable problem, which he formulates very early on in the book: "Live and invent. I have tried. I must have tried. Invent. It is not the word. Neither is live. No matter. I have tried." Malone wants to know what it is to be alive. His bodily functions tell him nothing, and so he is forced to make statements about living. But these statements are all inventions, because they each assume that the edited version of life is identical with life itself. However, as there is no other means of grappling with the problem, he must go on inventing. Invention enables the self to confront itself with its own image. This image can only be an appearance, and any presentation of the appearance will endow it with a meaning, and the meaning will be that of the appearance, not of the self. Toward the end, Malone interrupts the stories of Macmann and Lemuel with the words: "I had forgotten myself, lost myself." While life compels him to seek determinacy, he refutes any such determinacy in the stories, because he is fully aware of the purpose of the search. Thus the problem involved in "live and invent" remains insoluble, but it is through living and inventing that the self produces its own indeterminableness out of itself, by continually fictionalizing its various self-representations.

The fact that Malone regards this process as playing means that it can have no teleology that might endow the self with a final, determinate meaning. If it could, then the self would no longer be itself but the expression of something else. The only teleology there might be in the game is the rules of the game, which will condition the different possibilities of play. In the configurative meanings of the game, the self is present insofar as it is a possibility of meaning, and the more variations of play there are, the more prominently will the basic self emerge, increasingly overshadowing its individual manifestations. Malone is aware of this, too:

> My concern is not with me, but with another, far beneath me and whom I try to envy, of whose crass adventures I can now tell at last, I don't know how. Of myself I could never tell, any more than live or tell of others. How could I have, who never tried? To show myself now, on the point of vanishing, at the same time as the stranger, and by the same grace, that would be no ordinary last straw. Then live, long enough to feel, behind my closed eyes, other eyes close. What an end.

This is the subject matter of the third novel, linked to the necessity of exceeding the degree of consciousness already reached in the process of self-representation. The nameless narrator refers to no normal, external objective reality at all. At least Malone had spoken of the room in which he was lying and of different gestures which his situation still allowed him to make. In *The Unnamable* such relics of an outside world have disappeared altogether.

Malone could tell stories in order to relieve his boredom, though he knew that the material was drawn out of his own life, but for the unnamable this avoidance of the self is no longer possible through stories. His acute consciousness can see through the process even before it gets as far as story-telling. And yet the unnamable's record of his ceaseless monologue is permeated with recollections of Malone and other first-person narrators, and also with fragmentary references to other characters and voices. They act as spurs to his consciousness, so that the theme of this novel evolves out of the self-dissection of the first two. As far as the reader is concerned, the appearance of Malone, Molloy, and other characters offers a background of familiarity against which he can situate the searchings of the *The Unnamable*. *Malone Dies* showed that the attempt at self-observation through writing led inevitably to a process of fictionalization, and so this knowledge is already given to the unnamable. His writing therefore refers to the process of writing, and so the range of writing itself is extended. But where can such an extension possibly lead?

The beginning and the end of the novel speak of the unavoidability of self-confrontation. The phrasing in each case is similar and shows the impenetrability of the self and its compulsion to self-observation. The beginning is as follows: "Where now? Who now? When now? Unquestioning. I, say I. Unbelieving. Questions, hypotheses, call them that. Keep going, going on, call that going, call that on." The novel ends: "perhaps they have carried me to the threshold of my story, before the door that opens on my story, that would surprise me, if it opens, it will be I, it will be the silence, where I am, I don't know, I'll never know, in the silence you don't know, you must go on, I can't go on, I'll go on."

The "going-on" theme, which is echoed right through the novel, forms a kind of focal point for the highly conscious mind of the unnamable. Going on is an experience that defies integration and so acts as a constant stimulus for "hypotheses" about himself. Every attempt at self-representation is thus transformed into a fleeting movement of "hypotheses" that elude his grasp, so that he experiences himself under the inescapable compulsion of having to continue while knowing full well that whatever he writes down can be nothing but the record of an invented, or, to be more precise, a self-inventing character. Thus what cannot be integrated is shown to be the true reality, which defies the efforts of the conscious mind to grasp it. But if the conscious mind undergoes an experience which it is incapable of integrating, this very inability to integrate enables it to acknowledge its own unfathomableness. This is the source of the tension to which the narrator is exposed and which comes to the fore in all the various phases of his account. The unnamable frequently points out that he has invented the other characters—from Murphy to Watt, and from Molloy to Malone—so that through these ramifications of his ego he can objectify and so render explicable certain conditions of himself: "Inexistent, invented to explain I forget what. Ah yes, all lies, God and man, nature and the light of day, the heart's outpourings and the means of understanding, all invented, basely, by me alone, with the help of no one, since there is no one, to put off the hour when I must speak of me." But as the defensiveness of this passage shows, the self-inventions hit back at the unnamable: the "vice-exister(s)," as he calls them elsewhere, begin to usurp him, and indeed even to tell him "what I am like." And this means that he is now being invented by his own inventions; but he is aware of this process and so knows that all the insinuations of these characters which he records are themselves only a fiction. It is this knowledge alone which enables him to escape again from the state of being an invention.

The unnamable indicates this element of his knowledge by reproducing the statements his inventions make about him as quotations, so that he can accentuate the gap between what his characters want to make of him and what he really is. By writing, he cancels out the intention of what has been written, and so he frees himself from the conditional nature of his "gestalten." And as he cannot take up a "metastandpoint" from which to write, he can only elucidate himself by inverting the written through writing. And so he never ceases to observe how his invented characters conceive him. But in order to be able to present this awareness, he confronts himself with himself as an invention of one of his own (invented) characters. And he can then go on to show that any statement about him must be inapposite, because it cannot capture his real self.

Such inappropriateness is necessary as the incomprehension of the self can only be brought out by the endless succession of fictitious concepts of it. "My inability to absorb, my genius for forgetting, are more than they reckoned with. Dear incomprehension, it's thanks to you I'll be myself, in the end. Nothing will remain of all the lies they have glutted me with." Clearly, the basis of the self is that which cannot be integrated. Herein lies the teleology of the ceaseless process by which every view of the self is fictionalized. The unnamable is aware that the only chance of knowing the "incomprehension" of the self lies in seeing through his continual self-invention, which at the same time remains an indispensable process. In this way he discovers for himself his own inaccessibility, which he objectifies in his account by presenting every manifestation of himself in the state of its own obsolescence. Thus his account becomes more and more densely populated with indistinct "gestalten," which on the one hand arise out of his urge to transcend his own constitution as mere "matter," but on the other are constantly outstripped by the knowledge that they are only pictures of the unpicturable basis of the self.

At certain places in the narrative, this interaction becomes the actual subject matter—most strikingly when the conscious mind takes the invented characters to pieces: "Is there a single word of mine in all I say? No, I have no voice, in this matter I have none. That's one of the reasons why I confused myself with Worm. But I have no reasons either, no reason, I'm like Worm, without voice or reason, I'm Worm, no, if I were Worm I wouldn't know it, I wouldn't say it, I wouldn't say anything, I'd be Worm." It is impossible for the narrator to conceive himself. But this very impossibility prevents him from finishing his writing. If he were to stop, he would have to face up to the motive that guided his action (writing) and so to the whole conditionality of the situation from which the motive derived. He would then be identical with a conditioned action, and this is what his knowledge prevents him from being. By going on, he documents the fact that he is aware of the inaccessibility of his basic unprocessed self, for in the course of his compulsive self-reproduction, he constantly transcends the limitations of his individual self-perceptions. As the act of presentation turns these into fictions, he regards them as consciousness without reality. Such a qualification presupposes that he is in possession of a reality which cannot be integrated through presentation. That reality is himself. But in order to remain himself, he must always remain conscious of the fictions that condition his self-representation.

This consciousness is apparent in his retraction of every gestalt of himself the moment it has been formed. He thus deprives it of its representative character, but at the same time leaves it behind as one individual track of his life, which cannot be integrated into any overall order. It is this impossibility of integration that endows the track with its reality. And so by the continual retraction of his self-representations, he penetrates into the reality of his basic self. But as this base can never be formulated, he must go on. This is his one chance of becoming real—above all, because he has the consciousness necessary for the process: "I'm all these words, all these strangers, this dust of words, with no ground for their settling, no sky for their dispersing, coming together to say, fleeing one another to say, that I am they, all of them, those that merge, those that part, those that never meet, and nothing else, yes, something else, that I'm something quite different, a quite different thing, a worldless thing in an empty place."

The Beckett trilogy is based on an extraordinary paradox. The novels show how it becomes increasingly impossible for their narrators to conceive themselves—i.e., to find their own identity; and yet at the same time it is precisely this impossibility that leads them actually to discover something of their own reality. This paradox is very hard to unravel. If one regards becoming conscious, in Nietzsche's terms, as "a completely active reformation," it must be borne in mind that Beckett's characters are conscious of this process itself. Every activity of the conscious mind entails some sort of projection or assumption, insofar as this is the only way in which the given world can be made accessible for observation. In these novels, however, the conscious mind is not concerned with the outside world but with the activities of its own consciousness.

Once the conscious mind turns its attention to its own activities, it no longer functions as a means of translating outside data into comprehensible images; instead it focuses upon the projections and assumptions inherent in this process. But if these are shown up as preconditions for the functioning of consciousness, then the resultant image of the self will in fact be only an image of a preconditioned and so restricted manifestation of the self. As the heightened consciousness reduces all its images of the self to their nonrepresentative individuality, the self can only experience its own reality through an unending sequence of unintegrated and unintegratable images. For it is the distinguishing mark of reality that it resists integration, and the conscious mind turned in upon itself is in a position to discover this truth. The discovery takes place in a process which, in the trilogy itself, is described as "finality without end" (*Molloy*).

As regards the form of this process, we might turn . . . to Merleau-Ponty:

> My absolute contact with myself, the identity of being and appearance cannot be posited, but only lived as anterior to any affirmation. In both cases, therefore, we have the same silence and the same void. The experience of absurdity and that of absolute self-evidence are mutually implicatory, and even indistinguishable. The world appears absurd, only if a demand for absolute consciousness ceaselessly dissociates from each other the meanings with which it swarms, and conversely this demand is motivated by the conflict between those meanings. Absolute self-evidence and the absurd are equivalent, not merely as philosophical affirmations, but also as experiences. . . . A truth seen against a background of absurdity, and an absurdity which the teleology of consciousness presumes to be able to convert into truth, such is the primary phenomenon.
>
> (*Phenomenology of Perception*)

Absurdity and truth go hand in hand through Beckett's novels, and this brings us to the all-important question of how the reader can possibly respond to such texts—a question which we have avoided up to now, in order to bring out the fundamental nature of the problem confronting the reader. Unlike the Faulkner and Ivy Compton-Burnett novels, Beckett's trilogy deprives the reader not temporarily but totally of his usual privileged seat in the grandstand. These characters possess a degree of self-consciousness which the reader can scarcely, if at all, keep up with. Such texts act as irritants, for they refuse to give the reader any bearings by means of which he might move far enough away to judge them. The text forces him to find his own way around, provoking questions to which he must supply his own answers.

This technique can give rise to a wide range of reactions—the simplest being to close the book because one considers the text to be nonsense. Such a decision, however, implies that the reader believes he has reliable criteria for judging what is sense and what is nonsense. Among readers who do not regard the text as nonsense, a common reaction is to search for an allegorical meaning. If the text could be brought completely into line with an underlying allegory, then one would have regained one's distance from it. But there are two sides to such a process. Does the allegorical meaning explain the text, or does the explanation serve to restore the distance one does not want to lose? We tend to be ill at ease when there is something which resists understanding, and so although the allegorical interpretation may be serving the text, it may well be serving nothing but our own peace of mind. The reader will find that such an interpretation will forever be chasing after the compulsive self-reproduction of the characters, without being able to catch up with it; this does not necessarily mean that the trail is false, but it will demand constant readjustment, and the more corrections one has to make, the more conscious one becomes that the projected "allegory" cannot be equated with the intention of the text but is simply a "heuristic fiction" to help one over the distressing loss of distance.

D. Wellershoff maintains that the reader cannot leave Beckett's trilogy "in any direction with the consciousness of being supported by the author. The paradoxical involvement can only be broken off through an experience of self-evidence which Beckett provokes by refusing to give it" ("Failure of an Attempt at De-Mythologization," in *Samuel Beckett: A Collection of Critical Essays*). If each reader's own ideas fall short, because the personally conditioned meaning he ascribes to the text can only result in a limited comprehension of it, then those ideas themselves must stand in doubt. But which of us willingly allows his own basic concepts to become an object of scrutiny? For it must be realized that now comprehension means nothing less than evaluating the basis of the self that makes comprehension possible in the first place. In this way Beckett's text brings to the surface those presuppositions from which spring all operations of comprehension. And once the reader becomes conscious of these, he will find the very foundations of his knowledge beginning to shift beneath his feet. All those meanings which hitherto he had taken for granted, are now reduced to heuristic ideas, and these in turn can become the preconditions for new experiences of himself and of the outside world.

Whenever this occurs, the reader approaches the level of consciousness of Beckett's characters, and he only leaves it again when he seeks confirmation of his own experience and so restricts their "play" by imposing a meaning on it. If he enters into the movement of the text, he will find it difficult to get out again, for he will find himself increasingly drawn into the exposure of the conditions that underlie his own judgment. This conditionality as a subject for conscious reflection is all the more accentuated as the text precludes any standpoint from which it could be viewed as a whole.

In this process lies the esthetic dynamism of such texts: they resolutely resist all attempts at total comprehension, for this is the only way in which they can break down the barriers to the reader's contemplation of his own ideas. But if the reader refuses to allow the text to make its catalytic effect on his consciousness, this very decision brings about another effect: one can only release oneself from the text by trying to reduce the confusion of configurative meanings to a determinate, final meaning. In order to do this, the reader must stand at a distance from the text, but this distance, although it grants him a view, also ensures that his view will comprehend at most some of the possibilities of the text. And so in seeking a determinate meaning, the reader loses possibilities of meaning, and yet it is only through losing these possibilities that he can become aware of the freedom his faculty of understanding had enjoyed before he committed himself to passing judgments.

If Beckett's novels stimulate us into reconsidering our own preconceptions, then their intention can hardly be merely to represent the decadence of contemporary society. And yet they are often regarded as symptoms of decay, despair, and nihilism, even in cases where the reader's attitude shows that he would like to ascribe some lofty, if obscure significance to the texts. What prevents such readers from interpreting Beckett's characters and their world—in so far as they have a world—as purely and simply an expression of our agonized society, is the extraordinary activeness that typifies these characters. This is, at first sight, a surprising feature, as W. Sypher has pointed out: "We cannot speak of action in Beckett's novels, for the hero is fixed in what might be called a condition, which in some ways resembles the continuous texture in 'brutal' painting. The condition is not, however, inert; that is the puzzle. Inertia is to be expected" (*Loss of the Self*). This activeness cannot be counted among the symptoms of decay. And so a vital component of the characters directly contradicts a theory that would have them as nothing but a reflection of the pathology of contemporary society. They are simply too productive to symbolize the decadence of a social order.

This compulsive creativity, together with a progressive deformation, makes the characters seem quite inaccessible to the reader. They are not representative figures, and they indicate nothing outside themselves to which the reader might latch on, in order to participate in their situation. In their unceasing self-reproduction, they are themselves the source of a creativity which may, momentarily, take on a configurative gestalt, but will at once have any such meaning taken away from it. This creative force does not build up a world one can make oneself at home in (and if it did, there would be no further need for that creative force). On the contrary, it reveals the conditional nature of everything it has produced, purely because the product takes on the character of a gestalt which it must lose again if the creative force is to go on creating. The process is never ending, because everything produced is also conditioned, and because it is known to be conditional, it has to be discarded. And if the self is the basis of this creative force, then it is only logical that it should confront itself with the shadows of possibilities that bring each other forth and then drive each other away.

If the decadence theory is inadequate because it has to ignore the creative force of the characters, the question arises as to whether any theory can incorporate this force. Here we have a peak of consciousness that does not destroy activity but instead actually produces it, and as the raw material it works on is an inexhaustible potential (the self), one's explanatory theory would need to be as comprehensive as the process itself is open-ended. What Beckett has achieved in these novels is to set the self free to pursue a course of endless self-discovery. It is a process which a nuclear physicist might identify immediately, in terms that fit perfectly into our literary context, as a super-critical chain reaction.

Fiction, Myth, and Identity
in Samuel Beckett's Novel Trilogy

Leslie Hill

> *En fait, ce monde où nous vivons n'engendre plus de mythes nouveaux, et les mythes que la poésie semble fonder, s'ils ne sont pas objets de foi, ne révèlent finalement que le vide.*
>
> G<small>EORGES</small> B<small>ATAILLE</small>

Critical reception of Samuel Beckett's novel trilogy—*Molloy, Malone meurt* and *L'Innommable*—has often underlined the extent to which the novels appear to constitute themselves as a negation of their fictions and as a progressive elimination of their impulsion to narrate. It has often been felt that this process bears witness to an attempt to denude the speaking voice of the trilogy of all recourse to fictional self-narration and to attain to an experience of the self standing beyond language, not so much as an ineffable identity, but, rather, in the words of Olga Bernal, as "une conscience dénuée des repères des signes." As the same critic argues some pages later:

> L'entreprise difficile, impossible, qualifiée pur lui-même de "supplice," cette entreprise du héros de Beckett consiste à vouloir saisir l'homme en deçà de toute fiction. C'est la raison pour laquelle il n'arrive pas à se rendre présent, à être.

The purpose of this article will be to examine the validity of this standpoint and attempt to focus more closely upon the ambiguity and heterogeneity of Beckett's fiction.

But before turning to the novels themselves it is perhaps first necessary to consider the import for Beckett's fiction of that strange event in the writer's

From *Forum for Modern Language Studies* 13, no. 4 (October 1977). © 1977 by Leslie Hill.

career that may be seen here as an exemplary manifestation of the heterogeneity that the trilogy will explore: the author's decision henceforth to compose his novels in a foreign language. For it would be perhaps true to say that while many critics have often and convincingly examined Beckett's brilliance as a self-translator and the differing tonalities of his French and English versions, the possible impact of this change in language upon the nature of Beckett's writing has tended to be neglected.

One perceptive answer to this question has been advanced by Hugh Kenner, who, in the context of his generally post-Cartesian reading of Beckett, argues in the following terms:

> The words in which I carry out that unending dialogue that accompanies my conscious existence, these words cluster, ramify and so colour the unique person that I am as to precipitate within it what introspection knows as *self*. . . . New words then will seek to precipitate a modified self, though the person is the same. And a system of new words learned later in life with the assistance of the disciplined understanding will attract, if they are allowed to invest the consciousness, whatever potential selfhood floats closest to the ratiocinative.
>
> *(Samuel Beckett: A Critical Study)*

That a change of language should entail a modification of self and a revision of the position of self in language is a fact that perhaps any student of languages may confirm. But that this other selfhood should be closer to the ratiocinative areas of self is less certain. It is more a case of this shift in language permitting Beckett to approach the whole problem of language differently; it allows him to approach anew the crisis in language expounded in *Watt* from what may be termed a position of laterality. For the writer is no longer confronted with the starkness of his maternal tongue (already a problematic entity in the case of the Anglo-Irish author), and with the necessity, as in *Watt*, of using that language as a means of expressing its own collapse, but with the labile duplicity of another language, of language as radically other. Indeed, the other self that is composed by the fabric of a foreign tongue, in view of the distance that links the writer to the history of that language, will be, in quite an exemplary way, a fictional self, a self written with the words of others, into which the writer is reborn, confronted at every moment with a language that precedes his assumption of that language. And it is this renewed confrontation of a self with language that, beyond the possible biographic dimension of Beckett's writing, the trilogy will reenact, constituting itself as a constant tension between unstable Irish names and an anonymus French voice, in the scope of which the place of the author becomes unassignable, dispersed behind a series of fictional masks.

But such an awareness of the fictionality of self is not specific to the work of Beckett. On the contrary, many authors, including both Nietzsche and the logico-positivists, have insisted upon the illegitimate fashion in which philosophical discourse itself, working in complicity with the language of everyday communication, passes from what are the major syntactic categories of the Indo-European languages to the postulation of fixed metaphysical concepts. In this perspective the entire chain of concepts that have organised the thought of the West from Socrates to the present—terms such as "being," "self" or "identity"—can be considered as fictions deriving from the speculative use of what are autonomous and culturally relative grammatical structures. It may be suggested, indeed, that the notion of a unitary thinking consciousness preceding language—however negative and however tenuous this awareness may be—is an inversion of the process of a self composed and decomposed by the movement of language and enunciation, *a fortiori* when that self espouses a foreign language.

Such philosophical themes, however, interest Beckett's novels only insofar as they demonstrate the fictional basis of all language and of philosophic concepts, and, moreover, thus suggest an explanation of the philosophical references that have been traced in the trilogy. For indeed it would be untrue to say that such philosophical concepts as "self" derive mechanically from the languages of the West. Much more than this—and it is here that their relevance for the reading of the trilogy becomes apparent—they are necessary theoretical constructs without which thought would become impossible. As Nietzsche puts it, in what is one of his most suggestive posthumous texts:

> The *postulate of being* is necessary, in order that we may think and conclude: logic merely handles formulas for states that remain constant. For this reason this postulate would still lack conviction with regard to reality: the notion of "being" is part of our point of view. The "self" as being (—untouched by process and development).
>
> The *fictional world* of subject, substance, "reason" etc. is *necessary*: there exists in us a power to order, simplify, falsify, to make artificial distinctions. "Truth" is an urge to master the multiplicity of sensations.

Fiction becomes a frontier traced between meaning and nonmeaning; and beyond language, it may be argued, lies both for Beckett and for Nietzsche, not a curiously nonsubjective consciousness, but a *process*, the impact of which is not to suspend fiction but to displace it from its fixity, to project it into the "ceaseless unconditioned generation and passing away of line" (*Murphy*). It is within this context, where the movement through language involves the confrontation with the generation and evanescence of literature, that Beckett's trilogy may best be read.

Both Molloy and Moran, as has often been indicated, are quick to recognise the fictitious nature of their attempts at self-narration, and both point to their experience of language as a radical and inevitable affabulation of their reality as speaking selves. With the uneluctability of fate, of a "fatum," a thing said and determined long in advance, the persona of the trilogy, as he opens his mouth to speak, does no more than repeat, within fiction, the impossible fable of his disappearance from language:

> J'en sais ce que savent les mots et les choses mortes et ça fait une jolie petite somme, avec un commencement, un milieu et une fin, comme dans les phrases bien bâties et dans la longue sonate des cadavres. Et que je dise ceci ou cela ou autre chose, peu importe vraiment. Dire c'est inventer. Faux comme de juste. On n'invente rien, on croit inventer, s'échapper, on ne fait que balbutier sa leçon, des bribes d'un pensum appris et oublié, la vie sans larmes, telle qu'on la pleure.

Once the voice enters language, it is with the loss of any point of neutral origin or reality, and the experience of language becomes synonymous with the discrepancy between the need to enounce and the falsity of the enunciation. The drama of the trilogy is enacted in the confrontation between the impossibility of self-definition and the need nonetheless to comply with the "exigences d'une convention qui veut qu'on mente ou qu'on se taise" (*Molloy*).

But it is only, paradoxically, by entering the detour of fictional alienation represented by the discourse of self-exposition that the novels are able, by consuming the margins of this alienating falsity, to seize the fable of the self in its moments of dissolution. It is only with the mediation of self-exposition that Molloy gains an awareness of his own being, but this provisional solution is constructed only with the certainty of its own fragility. Self-definition suscitates more questions than it answers. As Molloy declares:

> Il faut faire attention, se poser des questions, par exemple celle de savoir si on est toujours, et si non, quand ça prit fin, et si oui combien de temps ça va durer encore, n'importe quoi qui vous empêche de perdre le fil du songe. Moi je me posais volontiers des questions, l'une après l'autre, rien que pour les contempler. Non, pas volontiers, par raison, afin de me croire toujours là. J'ap-

pelais ça réfléchir. Je réfléchissais presque sans arrêt, je n'osais pas m'arrêter.

The only stable awareness of being for Molloy comes from this dreamlike thread of self-contemplation in language and its questions; reflexion as an intellectual process is synonymous with self-reflexion in the mirror of language. The fictions of the trilogy can be seen as elaborating a representation of the "I" of the speaking voice from the perspective of language; identity, as Nietzsche argues, is part of that perspective. As Martin Esslin comments, "self-perception is a basic condition of our being; we exist because, and as long as, we perceive ourselves." And the vehicle of this self-perception is language itself, "cette rumeur qui se lève à la naissance et même avant." The self will thus remain divided and exterior to itself. For as Malone discovers, "à la veille de ne plus être, j'arrive à être un autre."

It would seem in this context that in order to attain to the evidentiality of its own being the speaking voice of the trilogy needs to supplement its own lack of image with the objectified mediation of a fictional persona. But these instances of mediation deprive the voice of the hope of evading language. They rather engage the voice on the slippery path of inescapable scission. Once that one stands within language, one is condemned to self-alienation; but one cannot stand beyond language because language has always preceded the attempt to move beyond it. Without language the voice would not have even the awareness of its absence from language. The voice can only plot its contours in terms of an oscillating dialectic of introjection and expulsion, of creation and destruction: "L'essentiel," writes Malone, "est de s'alimenter et d'éliminer, si l'on veut tenir. Vase, gamelle, voilà les pôles"; "oui," he continues, "j'essaierai de faire, pour tenir dans mes bras, une petite créature, à mon image, quoi que je dise. En la voyant mal venue, ou par trop ressemblante, je la mangerai."

In this way, the outer envelope of identity that the fictional persona confers upon the voice can but lead to a more radical process of dispersion. As Moran describes, in a famous passage:

Ce que je voyais ressemblait plutôt à un émiettement, à un effondrement rageur de tout ce qui depuis toujours me protégeait de ce que depuis toujours j'étais condamné à être. Ou j'assistais à une sorte de forage de plus en plus rapide vers je ne sais quel jour et quel visage, connus et reniés. Mais comment décrire cette sensation qui de sombre et massive, de grinçante et pierreuse, se faisait soudain liquide.

Such passages would seem to jettison the whole notion of fiction as alienation, and begin to inscribe within fiction the very process of dissolution that
lies beneath it. As the Unnamable declares, contradicting much of what is
said elsewhere:

> le plus simple est de dire que ce que je dis, ce que je dirai, si je
> peux, se rapporte à l'endroit où je suis, à moi qui y suis, malgré
> l'impossibilité où je suis d'y penser, d'en parler, à cause de la nécessité
> où je suis d'en parler, donc d'y penser peut-être un peu.

Although it would be hazardous indeed to attach any truth value to a statement of this kind, the reader is perhaps invited here to reconsider the nature
of Beckett's fictions, to ask whether the idea of "fictional alienation" is not
itself a fiction, and to concentrate upon the ambiguity of these fictions, and
the way in which they are "faux comme de juste."

Clearly, many critics have isolated, beneath the apparently derisory repetitions of these fictions, a mass of recurrent mythological motifs. Even while
the story of Molloy's encounter with Lousse is an ironically literal story of
a "chien écrasé," the reader is nonetheless "exposed to images of immense
compelling power, which, in spite of their sharpness of outline, remain impenetrable as though one heard a foreign language spoken with excessive
clarity" (Dieter Wellershoff). This language, suggests the same critic, is the
language of myth. Molloy himself declares, despite the fact that the domi-
nant tense of his narration is the imperfect, that "je parle au présent, il est
si facile de parler au présent, quand il s'agit du passé. C'est le présent mythologi-
que, n'y faites pas attention." The narrator of "Le Calmant" affirms in a
symmetrical fashion that "je mènerai néanmoins mon histoire au passé, comme
s'il s'agissait d'un mythe ou d'une fable ancienne, car il me faut ce soir un
autre âge, que devienne un autre âge celui où je devins ce que je fus."

The temporal structure of the trilogy is, in this way, far from being
linear. The anteriority of the past tense is disturbed considerably and, as
mythological allusions make it well up into the present, it becomes dependent
upon its moment of enunciation in the mouth of the speaker. The constant
interjections of the speaker throw doubt upon the authenticity of this past
tense, which is henceforth absorbed into the present. Inversely the future
tense remains perpetually present, as the monologue of the self is directed
towards a potential and unattainable future: "la recherche du moyen de faire
cesser les choses, taire sa voix, est ce qui permet au discours de se poursuivre."
The present tense of the speaking voice, seen traditionally in the context of
the philosophic "cogito" and the internal monologue as a mode of presence
and identity, is elided by Beckett's writing into a moment of hesitation, an

interstice suspended between a "too late" and a "not yet," just as life for
Malone is an interval between an impossible birth and an equally impossible
death. As one critic argues, "the sensation is . . ., paradoxically, a double
one of time expanding and contracting at the same time—expanding towards
absolute endlessness and slowing as it does so, contracting into absolute
simultaneity and . . . speeding up as it does so" (Ross Chambers). Time in
Beckett's trilogy becomes circular, and the presence of selfhood is eclipsed
in the shifting modalities of the past and the future, dimensions not of pure
awareness but of mythical recurrence. As Molloy laments:

> Ma vie, ma vie, tantôt j'en parle comme d'une chose finie, tantôt
> comme d'une plaisanterie qui dure encore, et j'ai tort, car elle est
> finie et elle dure à la fois, mais par quel temps du verbe exprimer
> cela?

In this manner Beckett's trilogy precipitates the notion of the transcendental self into a spiralling sequence of fictions, which, for all their fragility,
begin to circumscribe the enigma of their own origin, the "inénarrable
menuiserie qu'était mon existence." And it is this contradictory role that the
mythical temporality of the trilogy is called upon to play. For as Georges
Bataille suggests:

> La naissance que sans doute nous devons prêter à Molloy n'est pas
> celle d'une composition savante, mais la seule qui convienne à
> l'insaisissable réalité . . ., celle d'un mythe—monstrueux et sortant
> du sommeil de la raison. Deux vérités analogues ne peuvent prendre
> corps en nous que sous la forme d'un mythe, qui sont la mort
> et cette "absence d'humanité," qui est l'apparence vivante de la mort.
> De telles absences de réalité ne peuvent en effet être données dans
> les claires distinctions du discours, mais il est certain que ni la
> mort ni l'inhumanité, l'une et l'autre inexistantes, ne peuvent être
> tenues pour indifférentes à l'existence que nous sommes dont elles
> sont la limite, la toile de fond et la vérité dernière.
>
> ("Le Silence de Molloy")

The fictions of the trilogy demand thus to be read on two levels: as reified
and arbitrary linguistic fictions; but also as anagogic retracings of their own
enigmatic point of origin in the life of the self.

What emerges in Beckett's text once the notion of fictional alienation
is inverted can best be illustrated by citing an extract from "Le Calmant"
that follows the passage quoted earlier. The narrator writes:

> C'est à moi ce soir que doit arriver quelque chose, à mon corps,

> comme dans les mythes et métamorphoses, à ce vieux corps auquel
> rien n'est jamais arrivé, ou si peu, qui n'a jamais rien rencontré,
> rien aimé, rien voulu, dans son univers étamé, mal étamé, rien
> voulu sinon que les glaces s'écroulent, les planes, les courbes, les
> grossissantes, les rapetissantes, et qu'il disparaisse, dans le fracas
> de ses images.

The dissimulated metaphor of self, founded upon an analogy between syntax and reality, upon self-reflexion in the mirror of language, is supplanted by a process of metamorphosis, a metamorphosis that affects two essential areas of the self: his language and his body.

The linearity of narration, particularly in *Malone meurt*, becomes gradually consumed by an irregular oscillation between fiction and interjection, thematised by Malone as a "jeu" but commanded by a deep-seated experience of aporia. Language is unable to mirror the identity of self, but is fragmented into a sequence of discontinuous vocal instances, all of which are evanescent, and all of which retrace the difficulty of the voice's confrontation with language. "Le texte se transforme," writes G. Celati, "en une constellation de traces discontinues, d'accès soudains, de déviations et d'ironies non constructives, et, somme toute, en sérialité d'interpolations." It is this heterogeneity of enunciation that gives Beckett's prose its characteristic cadences. The unity of the sentence is broken up by the obsessive repetition of the comma, deferring the conclusion of sense into the zone of incompleted finitude that typifies the temporality of the mythological present. Language reirrupts into the trilogy not as a guarantee of a false identity but as sound. Works become marks of pure phonation, dissociated from reality and from self-expression, and yet "(inscrits) dans ma mémoire pour toujours."

> Oui, les mots que j'entendais, et je les entendais très bien, ayant
> l'oreille assez fine, je les entendais la première fois, et même encore
> la seconde, et souvent jusqu'à la troisième, comme des sons purs,
> libres de toute signification. . . . Et les mots que je prononçais moi-
> même et qui devaient presque toujours se rattacher à un effort
> de l'intelligence, souvent ils me faisaient l'effet d'un bourdonne-
> ment d'insecte.
>
> (*Molloy*)

The text is not written according to the continuity of a single consciousness expressing itself in language, but according to the babble of the "deux pitres, entre autres" who inhabit the dispersion of the speaking voice.

Parallel to this return of language into the text as a "body of fundamental sounds," the body of the speaking self reemerges into the text. This body is no longer the body of a self assured of its own identity, constructed hierarchically around consciousness as source and figurehead of being, but a body that bears the stigmata of the original and enigmatic confrontation with language, just as the voice of *Comment c'est* bears the wounds of his meeting with Pim. As Moran contemplates his own image in language, as in earlier novels Sam had looked upon Watt over the fence, and Murphy upon Mr. Endon over the chess-board, it is this other body that becomes visible, recalling to the self the nature of his existence, the cruelty of his birth into language:

> Je voyais alors une petite boule montant lentement des profondeurs,
> à travers des eaux calmes, unie d'abord, à peine plus claire que
> les remous qui l'escortent, puis peu à peu visage, avec les trous
> des yeux et de la bouche et les autres stigmates, sans qu'on puisse
> savoir si c'est un visage d'homme ou de femme, jeune ou vieux,
> ni si son calme aussi n'est pas un effet de l'eau qui le sépare du jour.

Clearly this body is not the same as that of the organised, articulate framework of selfhood, but another, which doubles the first without being identical to it. It is the body considered as the irreducible capital of existence, as a surface of inscription on which the language of self imprints its wounds, and upon which the various figures of the trilogy are "une suite ou plutôt une succession de phénomènes locaux" (*Malone meurt*). This body loses its homogeneous unity, and is devoured by its indeterminacy; it becomes a contradictory site of languages, a "longue folie" (*Molloy*) from which all identity has been expunged, and where the shattered images of the self reveal the cacophony of fragmentation:

> Je me lève, sors, et tout est changé. Ma tête se vide de sang, de
> toutes parts m'assaillent les bruits des choses s'évitant, s'unissant,
> volant en éclats, mes yeux cherchent en vain des ressemblances,
> chaque point de ma peau crie un autre message, je chavire dans
> l'embrun des phénomènes.
>
> (*Molloy*)

The secure distinctions between characters are undermined. All the fictional selves of the trilogy are reinscribed upon the flesh of "cet impensable ancêtre dont on ne peut rien dire," who will figure in the trilogy as the Unnamable, as "une grande boule lisse," and who, if he can be said to precede language, does so only as the physical condition of speech, as the "matière, matière, tripotée sans cesse en vain" upon which "le pus bienfaisant de la raison" has traced its "réseaux de fistules" (*L'Innommable*). The voice of the trilogy is the exteriority of a process of negativity to which selfhood owes its birth, and which is itself "dans son essence anonyme" (*Molloy*); it is around the original and enigmatic confrontation of a body and a language that Beckett's fiction turns, passing, as I have suggested, through another tongue — French — in order to narrate this heterogeneous encounter.

It is in this way that far from being an attempt to attain to an unpredicated state of being or nonbeing, Beckett's trilogy marks an effort to circumscribe, within fiction, the blank enigma of its own origin, of that story which, if it is literally fundamental to the very nature of selfhood, nonetheless stands beyond the grasp both of the self and of the discourse of self-definition. It is by exploiting the shifting heterogeneity and ambiguity of the adventure of writing that the trilogy is able to reinscribe this unapproachable centre, repeating endlessly its contours in the impossible pursuit of the mysterious poverty of birth. In the words of the voice of the *Textes pour rien*:

> C'était un conte, un conte pour enfants, ça se passait sur un rocher, au milieu de la tempête, la mère était morte et les mouettes venaient s'écraser contre le fanal, Joe se jeta à l'eau, c'est tout ce que je me rappelle, un couteau entre les dents, fit le nécessaire et revint, c'est tout ce que je me rappelle ce soir, ça finissait bien, ça commençait mal et ça finissait bien, tous les soirs, une comédie, pour enfants. Oui, j'ai été mon père et j'ai été mon fils, je me suis posé des questions et j'ai répondu de mon mieux, je me suis fait redire, soir après soir, la même histoire, que je savais par coeur sans pouvoir y croire.

The Self-Multiplying Narrators of *Molloy, Malone Dies,* and *The Unnamable*

Charlotte Renner

In the unpublished novel "Dream of Fair to Middling Women" (1932), Samuel Beckett asserts, "The experience of the reader shall be between the phrases, in the silence communicated by the intervals, not in the terms of the statement." This rare statement of aesthetic purpose may be applied to Beckett's other work in more than one way. On the most obvious level, Beckett seems to be anticipating by many years theories recently propounded by Wolfgang Iser, Stanley Fish and others pertaining to the reception of fictional texts. Beckett's "intervals" may correspond to the "gaps" which, according to Iser, separate not only one sentence, paragraph or chapter from another, but also the reader's expectations from the author's ongoing description of events. Anyone who has read even one of Beckett's novels will probably agree that he seems intentionally to create more "intervals" of many kinds than even the most astute reader is prepared to fill. That may be why the trilogy of *Molloy, Malone Dies* and *The Unnamable* is one of the most difficult yet rewarding works of modern literature. The reader must attempt not only to connect the cryptically comic statements made by the several narrating voices in each volume, but also to bridge the larger "intervals" separating one multivocal volume from the next.

Beckett's trilogy may seem to be without structural precedent in literary history. In some ways, it is. But in an effort to ease somewhat the great difficulty of all three novels, we may associate them with other more conventional fictions self-consciously narrated by more than one character. This

From *The Journal of Narrative Technique* 11, no. 1 (Winter 1981). © 1981 by *The Journal of Narrative Technique.*

approach demands that we treat the trilogy as a continuous fiction narrated by more than one voice. But it also allows us to see how each of the novels is, in its own way, a choral narration.

I will refer in passing, throughout this essay, to several multi-vocal fictions which predate Beckett's work: James Hogg's *Private Memoirs and Confessions of a Justified Sinner*, Brontë's *Wuthering Heights*, Dickens's *Bleak House* and Faulkner's *Absalom, Absalom!*. I choose these works for the sake of comparison because they, like Beckett's trilogy (and unlike, for example, Joyce's *Ulysses*) are narrated by choruses of characters conscious of their collective responsibilities to a reading or listening audience. In general, we can say that this consciousness tends to become particularly acute in modern fictions, in which narrating characters collaborate most fully to invent, as well as discover, the truth about a central hero or heroine. By the end of Faulkner's novel, Quentin Compson and Shreve McCannon are granted freedoms reserved, in most nineteenth-century fiction, for the novelist's persona: the rights to generate imagery and irony, to read the minds of other characters, and even to invent a nonnarrating character, the lawyer who, according to them, contributes to Sutpen's downfall.

Analogous but much broader liberties are extended to Beckett's narrators who, in a way I wish to examine, actually invent and reinvent *themselves* in the course of their various narrations. In a recent article, Stephen M. Ross makes a distinction that will be useful to us. "Mimetic voice," he proposes, "is that collection of features in a work's discourse which prompts readers to regard a particular portion of the work's total discourse as the utterance of an imagined person (character, narrator, 'author')." "Textual voice," on the other hand, "is the result of elements in the physical text that . . . prompt or allow the reader to regard the printed text as a source for signification" ("Voice in Narrative Texts: The Example of *As I Lay Dying*"). As textual voices, Molloy and his successors are comically unable to conduct normal conversation: "And this is perhaps one of the reasons I was so untalkative," Molloy explains, "I mean this trouble I had in understanding not only what others said to me but also what I said to them." Beckett's narrators are incapable of interlocution because they construct themselves exclusively from written, printed, words. They exist in no other form. Whereas earlier multi-vocal novels are narrated by mimetic voices telling stories to each other about each other, Beckett's textual voices create themselves and each other by the stories they tell in solitude.

Ironically, Molloy and company remember less about themselves than, for example, Quentin and Shreve learn about the inscrutable Thomas Sutpen. "The truth is I don't know much," Molloy admits. Thus Beckett deepens the epistemological dilemma underlying most choral narrations. At the same time, however, he embraces the spectre of solipsism that earlier authors, whose characters are permitted to correct each other's impressions, avoid. For Beckett, "the individual is a succession of individuals; the world being a projection of the individual consciousness (the objectification of the individual's will, Schopenhauer would say), the pact must be continually renewed, the letter of safe conduct brought up to date" (S. Beckett, *Proust*). If we understand each volume of the trilogy to be "a letter of safe conduct" written by one narrator about his transformation into a series of other selves, we can see why the resulting chronicle must be not only multi-vocal, but multi-textual as well.

Because Beckett redirects the narrative chorus away from fictional biography and towards a new kind of autobiographical fiction, it is impossible to ignore the connections between Beckett's life and those of his characters. Hugh Kenner, for example, points out the geographical similarities between Molloy's Bally and Beckett's Irish homestead, and between Moran's town and Beckett's adopted France. Deirdre Blair finds *Malone Dies* to be "the most autobiographical of all Beckett's fictions." But of course these and other autobiographical details are not meant to tell the story of Samuel Beckett. On the contrary, they allow Beckett to become anonymous by transferring his history, property and family to a series of fictional avatars, whom he then proceeds to deprive of *their* histories, property and families. In this way, the implied author of the trilogy reverses the autobiographical process, by stripping the historical novelist of his historicity.

Thus Beckett takes multi-vocal fiction into unexplored territory. Yet he does so by following some familiar paths. In many multi-vocal novels, the narrative chorus consists of one or more pairs of antithetical characters. Bronte's Lockwood and Nelly, Dickens's "author" and Esther, Faulkner's Quentin and Shreve—all report events from complementary perspectives. Even as these voices are joined by others, the choruses continue to break down into duets between tellers and listeners, insiders and outsiders, reporters and interpreters of events. In each case, the reader must meditate between two points of view to arrive at a third synthetic vision of the hero.

As I hope to show, Beckett adapts this multi-vocal biographical strategy for use by his fictional autobiographers. Each text in the trilogy is narrated by or about pairs of antithetical avatars. But whereas in earlier novels the complementarity of narrating characters tends to introduce objectivity into the narrative process, the trilogy depends upon the power of the subjective self to imagine rather than discover its antithesis, with whom it eventually merges. Beckett's characters do not merely complement each other; they cancel each other. Yet in so doing they create a third narrating hero: "And on the threshold of being no more I succeed in being another. Very pretty," Malone remarks.

Conventionally, the members of a narrative chorus may be distinguished by their respective styles of discourse. Lockwood preserves Nelly's highly colloquial language, thereby allowing us to distinguish between her attitudes towards Heathcliff and his own. The "author" of *Bleak House* relies on metaphor to tell us what Esther's plain prose cannot. Even when not all the facts are known about a hero or heroine, it is possible to arrange the stories of other characters so as to multiply the interpretations of what *is* known. For example, Rosa's gothic descriptions and Mr. Compson's classical imagery pose two alternative responses to the events in *Absalom, Absalom!*

We may say, then, that several multi-vocal fictions written before Beckett's trilogy are based on the assumption that the style of one's discourse exposes the bias, or boundaries, of one's perception. Beckett takes this premise one giant step further by implying that *all* language, whatever its style, inevitably falsifies reality: "Live and invent," Malone says. "I have tried. I must have tried. Invent. It is not the word. Neither is live." Marlow and Quentin resort frequently to symbolic imagery to suggest what cannot be explained. But Beckett's narrators know their very voices to be obstacles in the path of unspeakable truths:

> And I did not say, Yet a little while at the rate things are going, etc. but that resembled perhaps what I would have said, if I had been able. In reality I said nothing at all, but I heard a murmur, something gone wrong with the silence, and I pricked up my ears, like an animal I imagine, which gives a start and pretends to be dead.
>
> *(Molloy)*

To tell the truth about himself, each narrator must hear more acutely than the last this practically inaudible, paradoxically nonverbal murmur of reality, and to transcribe the murmur for us. At the end of *Molloy*, Moran says, "I have spoken of a voice, a voice telling me things. I was getting to know it better now, to understand what it wanted." To Malone the voices, now plural, speak more clearly—but only when he himself is speechless: "When I stop, the noises begin again, strangely loud, those whose turn it is. So that I seem to have again the hearing of my boyhood." Finally, the Unnamable exhorts the voice to become singularly his: "Let it go through me at last, the right one, the last one, his who has none, by his own confession." As we shall see, the appropriately named Unnamable comes closer than any other narrator to hearing and imitating this interior paradoxically silent sound of truth.

If, as Beckett implies, silence "speaks" more truthfully than words, that is because language—especially written prose—upholds a view of life as a linear, chronological sequence of events. The principles of grammar and syntax force us to place every human thought or action in the past, present, or future. Moreover, to speak consistently in the first, second, or third person suggests that one's identity is invulnerable to mutation. But for Beckett, the self is always in the process of being defined and redefined, and the reality of the world is contingent upon one's ever-changing point of view. The "individual," therefore, must be seen as "the seat of a constant process of decantation, decantation from the vessel containing the fluid of future time, sluggish, pale, monochrome, to the vessel containing the fluid of past time, agitated and multicoloured by the phenomena of its hours" (*Proust*).

To reflect what Beckett sees as the atemporality of life, the trilogy is not only, like most multi-vocal fictions, nonchronological; it is in fact antichronological. In other words, it reverses the traditional order of artistic composition. In most fictions, the implied author is understood to be prerequisite to the invention of narrating characters. In fact, novels like *Bleak House*, in which the "author" also narrates, are normally introduced by the "author" who then proceeds to share the story with one or more fictional raconteurs. In Beckett's trilogy, however, the "author" (or, in Bernal's terms, the "Je") has no existence prior to inventing its mutable incarnations. This paradox is as difficult for Molloy and Moran as it is for us. To signify his inexistent creator, Moran invents Youdi who, with the help of various emissaries, propels the novel forward by instructing Moran to find his antithesis in Molloy. Yet as Moran knows, Youdi dwells within him, as well: "For the voice I listen to needs no Gaber to make it heard. For it is within me and exhorts me to continue to the end the faithful servant I have always been." Thus the authorial Youdi allows himself to be invented, and constantly reinvented, by and as his creations. "For there was this about Youdi," Moran observes meaningfully, "that he changed his mind with great facility." Significantly, *Molloy* is the only text in the trilogy to be extracted by its narrators from this imaginary dictator. Having arranged for the "decantation" of Molloy into Moran, "Youdi" is able to emerge as a self-motivated Malone.

If we understand Molloy and Moran to be the future and past selves of Malone, we can see why the title of Malone's narrative—the only one to contain both subject and verb—is written in the present tense. But *Malone Dies* is not a true sequel to *Molloy*; rather, it is *Molloy* rewritten by a new "author." In fact, at strategic points in his story, Malone lapses into one

of his earlier voices. For example, Malone's admission that "I do not remember
how I got here. In an ambulance perhaps, a vehicle of some kind certainly"
echoes Molloy's opening statements: "I don't know how I got here. Perhaps
in an ambulance, certainly a vehicle of some kind." Malone interrupts his
story at another point with a seeming non sequitur "When it rained, when
it snowed." But these words, too, originated with Molloy: "When it rained,
when it snowed, when it hailed, then I found myself faced with the following dilemma." It would appear, then, that while the identities of narrating
characters are fragile, vulnerable to collision or change, their voices remain
intact, as it were, capable of accumulating and resurfacing in later texts—
perhaps to mark those points at which the new narrator's fiction runs parallel
to his former life.

These iterative sentences, and the reuse of tell-tale props like bicycles
and greatcoats, argue the existence of a paradigmatic tale or, in structuralist
terms, the "mobile fragment," subject to renarration or revison by each new
autobiographer in the trilogy. The earliest and most succinct summary of
it may be found in Molloy's story of "A" and "C":

> So I saw A and C going slowly towards each other, unconscious
> of what they were doing. It was on a road remarkably bare.
> . . . The town was not far. It was two men, unmistakably, one
> small and one tall. They had left the town, first one, then the
> other, and then the first, weary or remembering a duty, had re-
> traced his steps. The air was sharp for they wore greatcoats. They
> looked alike, but no more than others do. At first a wide space
> lay between them. . . . But the moment came when together
> they went down into the same trough and in this trough finally
> met.

The parallels between this fable and the plot of *Molloy* are hard to ignore.
Like A and C, Molloy and Moran (both of whom ride bicycles and wear
greatcoats) were antithetical in appearance. Neither A and C nor Molloy and
Moran can see each other; the "wide space" separating A from C corresponds
not only to the fictional landscape of *Molloy* but also to the textual space between the two narratives of that novel. But the fable tells us how to bridge
that gap, how to transcend the myopia of the narrators and imagine their
symbolic "meeting" "in the same trough" of immobility and physical decay.
For as Moran himself supposes, "my own natural end, and I was resolved
to have no other, would it not at the same time be his?"

I am suggesting that the story of A and C is a kind of dramatic pro-
logue, a shadow-play summary of the narrative activity to follow. All three

of the trilogy's narrators will tell stories about two complementary characters whose identities coalesce. Because they are independent authors (rather than mere scribes), Malone and the Unnamable will recognize the fictiveness of their versions of A and C. Moreover, they will be free to rewrite Molloy's little story in their ways. For them, as for the reader, such storytelling is a symbolic way to define and redefine oneself. But for Molloy, whose author is absent, A and C are *real*; they exist as fellow fictions, images (though unrecognizable to Molloy) of Molloy and Moran. Having told the story of A and C, Molloy then proceeds with Moran to act it out.

The most important fact about A and C is that they begin by being unconscious of each other: they do not know that they are meeting until after they have "met" and, presumably, merged: "to say they knew each other, no, nothing warrants it," Molloy admits. But Molloy looks forward to a time when, perhaps at the end of the larger novel, "they will know each other, even in the depths of the town." I take this to mean that Molloy's dream-like vision of A and C will come true only when it is reenacted by Molloy and Moran. As A and C originate from the same town, but become separated by geographical barriers, Molloy and Moran originate from the same authorial imagination, but reside in separate regions, separate texts. Being versions of the same self, they cannot encounter each other directly, as the Molloy and Moran we know. But each can meet, within his own text, an image of the other. And these internal images are based on the characters of A and C.

These relationships, between A and C and between them and Molloy and Moran, are so complete and convoluted that it is almost impossible to avoid confusion. (That may be Beckett's point about one's images of oneself.) Even Molloy gets muddled: "I felt the first stars tremble, and my hand on my knee and above all the other wayfarer, A or C, I don't remember, going resignedly home." However, we may at least begin to sort out the story by observing that Molloy sees in "C" the distorted reflection of himself:

> It seemed to me he wore a cocked hat. I remember being struck by it, as I wouldn't have been, for example by a cap or by a bowler. I watched him recede, overtaken (myself) by his anxiety, at least by an anxiety which was not necessarily his, but of which as it were he partook. Who knows if it wasn't my own anxiety overtaking him.

It is important to note that the correspondence between Molloy and C is not exact. C's stick, for example, suggests not Molloy, but Malone, who will preserve from what we may call the four-way collision of A, C, Molloy and Moran, the artifacts suggesting his origins. On the one hand, C's hat is remarkably like Molloy's:

> But the hat, a town hat, an old-fashioned town hat, which the least gust would carry far away. Unless it was attached under the chin, by means of a string or elastic. I took off my hat and looked at it. It is fastened, it has always been fastened, to my buttonhole, always the same buttonhole, at all seasons by a long lace. I am still alive then. That may come in useful.

Similarly, A is similar, but not identical, to Moran: "He was bareheaded, wore sand shoes, and smoked a cigar." Molloy also thinks he sees something following him: "A pomeranian I think, but I don't think so. I wasn't sure at the time and I'm still not sure, though I've hardly thought about it." At the beginning of his narrative, Moran smokes a cigar; at the end, he sees a dog—not a pomeranian, but a sheepdog. Molloy is mistaken about that. But then, as he admits, "I saw him only darkly." And as Moran says in another connection, "the falsity of terms does not imply that of the relation." The similarities between Molloy and C, and Moran and A, are clear; the differences may be attributed to Molloy's lack of information about himself, and also to his fertile imagination.

Although most critics agree that Moran becomes, in some sense, Molloy, none has attempted to describe the process by which this transformation occurs as a series of events. In order to become one with Molloy, Moran must first destroy his image of himself, who may also be Molloy's "A" in disguise:

> He was on the small side, but thick-set. He wore a thick navy-blue suit (double-breasted) of hideous cut and a pair of outrageously wide black shoes, with the toe caps higher than the uppers. . . . He had a narrow-brimmed dark blue felt hat on his head, with a fish hook and an artificial fly stuck in the band. . . . But all this was nothing compared to the face which I regret to say vaguely resembled my own, less the refinement of course, same little abortive mustache, same little ferrety eyes, same paraphimosis of the nose, and a thin red mouth that looked as if it was raw from trying to shit its tongue.

A "little later," Moran finds his double "stretched on the ground, his head in a pulp. . . . He no longer resembled me." Ludovic Janvier observes that "this encounter must have been the occasion of one of those rebirths through which Moran was able to give himself up completely to the hastening of the transformation—Molloy." What Janvier doesn't mention is that the man whom Moran kills was searching for another man, a version of Molloy's "C," who had already crossed Moran's path:

> He wore a coat much too heavy for the time of year and was leaning on a stick so massive, and so much thicker at the bottom than the top, that it seemed more like a club. He turned and we looked at each other for some time in silence. . . . His face was pale and noble, I could have done with it.

After handling the stranger's stick, which he seems to covet as much as his face, Moran watches his visitor walk away. But he does not see him disappear completely: he only *wishes* he "could have stood there, looking after him." Molloy had similarly been unable to let his image of Moran vanish: "He disappeared, the smoking object in his hand. Let me try to explain. From things about to disappear I turn away in time." (Yet he eerily *imagines* an encounter between himself and A not unlike the one Moran describes: "He hears my cries, turns, waits for me. . . . He is a little frightened of me, a little sorry for me. . . . He is kind, tells me of this and that and other things.") Molloy cannot lose sight of "A," and Moran cannot lose sight of "C" because each must, in time, become the other. Furthermore, Moran refuses to tell his blue-suited visitor where to find the C-like character. In fact, he kills rather than reveal the latter's whereabouts:

> To cut a long story short he wanted to know if I had seen an old man with a stick pass by. He described him. Badly. The voice seemed to come to me from afar. No, I said. . . . He thrust his hand at me. I have an idea I told him once again to get out of my way.

Moran must preserve "C" from harm for the same reason that he kills "A" — so as to merge with Molloy. For it is Molloy who must kill *his* image of himself before the final "decantations" can symbolically take place.

We may now understand why, in his narrative, Molloy encounters only one of the men who had visited Moran: the other, the heavy-set "A," had already been killed. It is possible that A's prey, the man with a stick, reappears to Molloy smelling of the smoke from Moran's fire or his cigar: "A total stranger. Sick with solitude probably. I say charcoal-burner, but really I don't know. I see smoke somewhere." Molloy is as disgusted by his double — "the dirty old brute" — as Moran was by him. "So," Molloy says, "I smartly freed a crutch and dealt him a good dint on the skull." As "A" was destroyed, so now is C, leaving Moran free to become Molloy and Molloy free to assimilate Moran.

If, as it appears, Moran's adventures antedate Molloy's—if, that is, Moran kills A before Molloy kills C—why does Molloy's narrative come first? Critics offer several answers to that question. According to Edith Kern, "Disregard for chronology should not surprise us in an author as obsessed with the absurdity of logic as is Beckett." Kern believes that Beckett, in the form of Youdi's messenger, urges Molloy to "re-arrange his story so what was now the beginning is nearly the end"—all in the interest, according to Kern, of "artistic appeal" ("Moran-Molloy: The Hero as Author"). Olga Bernal, on the other hand, proposes that "the reversal of chronological order reflects Molloy's own forgetfulness and irrationality." My own view is that the structure of *Molloy* is not under Molloy's control. Rather, it follows from Beckett's definition of the self, cited earlier, as "a constant process of decantation" of the "fluid of future time" into the "fluid of past time." Moran is not Molloy's sole creator; he invents, in "C," only one of several possible Molloys: "The fact was there were three, no, four Molloys. He that inhabited me, my caricature of the same, Gaber's and the man of flesh and blood somewhere awaiting me." The fifth one, Youdi's Molloy who opens the novel, is not within Moran's range of vision. In other words, the narrators named Molloy and Moran are introduced not in the order of their creation, but in such a way as to force the emergence from them of a third persona. If Moran's narrative were to come first, it would appear that, as John Fletcher argues, Molloy is simply an older Moran. As it is, however, the relationship between the two characters is considerably more complex than that. Since we meet Molloy before we meet Moran, we cannot merely allow the former to take the latter's place in our minds. Instead, we must imagine their synthesis, and the formation of a new textual voice.

The division of *Molloy* into two texts emphasizes the fact that neither Molloy nor Moran is the "author" of the entire novel. As Moran explains, "what I was doing was neither for Molloy, who mattered nothing to me, nor for myself, of whom I despaired, but on behalf of a cause which, while having need of us to be accomplished, was in its essence anonymous, and would subsist, haunting the minds of men, when its miserable artisans would be no more." In contrast, Malone portrays himself as an avatar of the "author," fully in control of his text: "This time I know where I am going," he insists, "it is no longer the ancient night, the recent night. Now it is a game, I am going to play." By "playing," Malone hopes to pass the time remaining until his impending death with which the novel, he reasons, will mercifully conclude. But every game has its rules. If his death is to be final, Malone must be careful not to retrace the steps leading to his original emergence from Molloy and Moran: he must not, in other words, retell the story of

A and C. "They will not be the same kind of stories as hitherto, that is all," he promises. Furthermore, if his death is to be *his*, he must sustain his identity throughout the novel; his fictional characters must remain as distinct from him as they are from each other. In many ingenious ways, Malone tries desperately to observe these simple rules. But for reasons we shall explore, he cannot help breaking one or the other of them at every turn.

In Sapo, Malone hopes to have invented a nonautobiographical hero. But the distance between author and fiction constantly threatens to close, and when it does, Malone must interrupt the story with some remark reminding himself and us of its fictiveness. For example, after reporting that Sapo "made a practice of mental arithmetic," and that "the figures then marshalling in his mind thronged it with colour and forms," Malone is obliged to say, after a pause represented by space on the page, "What tedium." Similarly, Malone suppresses his autobiographical impulse when he makes this important correction: "Sapo had no friends—no, that won't do. Sapo was on good terms with his little friends. . . ." Malone must also avoid the temptation to enter Sapo's mind or to put his words into Sapo's mouth: "The market. The inadequacy of exchanges between rural and urban areas had not escaped the excellent youth. He had mustered, on this subject, the following considerations, some perhaps close to, others no doubt far from, the truth. In his country, the problem—no, I can't do it."

As long as Sapo remains younger than Malone, Malone is able, by constantly correcting himself, to keep Sapo's story separate from his own. But the older Sapo gets, the more he resembles Malone—especially in the way his "gull's eyes" gravely see the "unconquerable dark" even in the midst of natural beauty and light. Soon, Malone realizes that his voice and Sapo's may have already united: ". . . I write about myself with the same pencil and in the same exercise book as about him. It is because it is no longer I . . . but another whose life is just beginning." To drive a new wedge between himself and Sapo, Malone allows Sapo to drift away from his own family (which we assumed to resemble Malone's) and into the Lambert family. By showing Sapo's incomprehensible attraction to the repugnant and violent Lamberts, Malone once more distinguishes himself from his fictional persona. But eventually even this distance disappears. In the same paragraph which shows Malone's growing sympathy for Mrs. Lambert, we learn that Sapo is going away—apparently because Malone cannot afford to become attached to Sapo's friends:

> Her mind was a press of formless questions, mingling and crumbling
> limply away. Some seemed to have to do with her daughter, that

minor worry, now lying sleepless in her bed, listening. . . . It was only the next day, or the day after, that she decided to tell her what Sapo had told her, namely that he was going away and would not come back.

When Sapo leaves the Lamberts, he leaves the novel. But so, it seems, does Malone:

I have spent two unforgettable days of which nothing will be ever known . . . except that they brought me the solution and conclusion of the whole sorry business, I mean the business of Malone (since that is what I am called now) and of the other, for the rest is no business of mine. And it was, though more unutterable, like the crumbling away of two little heaps of finest sand, or dust, or ashes, of unequal size, though diminishing together as it were in ratio, if that means anything, and leaving behind them, each in its own stead, the blessedness of absence.

Like A and C, and Molloy and Moran, Malone and Sapo disappear not from, but into, each other.

And yet a voice remains to tell us of this cancellation. And this new temporarily anonymous narrator, being an amalgam of all earlier voices, is more authorial than any of its predecessors. That is to say that, unlike Molloy, Moran and Malone, for whom birth and death are actual events, this voice implicitly understands its birth and death to be metaphors for the self-mutation of the absent "author" for whom it speaks. Malone had spoken figuratively of his birth "from the world that parts at last its labia and lets me go" — into death, we presume. But it is not until he merges with Sapo, his version of himself as child, that he extends the image: "Yes, an old foetus, that's what I am now, hoar and impotent." Later, in a fantasy about a little girl who would mother him, he explains the pun: "Take it easy Malone, you old whore." These references to himself as both "foetus" and "whore" are not casual figures of speech; rather they follow from the narrator's revelation that his fictional personae are not only the illegitimate issue, but also the reincarnations, of himself. The "rules" of his game must, then, be revised. Instead of attempting to remain distinct from his fictions, the narrator will now allow himself to die in giving birth to another self, whom he will later kill:

Yes, a little creature, I shall try and make a little creature, to hold in my arms, a little creature in my image, no matter what I say.

> And seeing what a poor thing I have made, or how like myself,
> I shall eat it.

Since the narrator has already "eaten" both Sapo and Malone, this new "little creature" must be renamed, after both of its predecessors. "Macmann" sounds like "Malone." But is also indirectly linked to "sapo," as "homo" is to "sapiens."

The metaphorical intersection of birth, death and sex is also semantically suggested by Beckett's narrators. If Molloy "dies" by uniting with Moran and Malone "dies" by merging with Sapo, then death must be analogous with (but not equivalent to) sexual activity, which brings about the "birth" of another narrator. These double and triple entendres are more numerous in Malone's discourse than in Molloy's or Moran's, and they are most explicitly exploited by the Unnamable who, upon the "death" of Mahood and the "birth" of Worm, becomes at once the mother and child of himself:

> I'll have my bellyful of mammals, I can see that from here, before
> I wake. Quick, give me a mother and let me suck her white,
> pinching my tits.

If, as the trilogy suggests, language is false because arbitrary, the richer and more paradoxical its semantic reverberations, the less mendacious a written text will be. At no time, however, will a spoken or printed word transmit the "truth" about its speaker, or writer.

Why, then, do Beckett's narrators talk, or write, at all? They do so not to tell the "truth" but to invent it; by writing, each narrator brings himself and another into the reader's mind. Beckett's functionalist view of language anticipates very recent psychoanalytic theory about utterance and selfhood. The relationships between Molloy and Moran, Malone and Sapo, and the Unnamable and Mahood roughly parallel "the dual relationship between *moi* and other" described by Jacques Lacan. Insofar as they "issue" from each other, each of Beckett's narrators is like a child who is, for Lacan, "an absolute subject in a totally intransitive relationship to the world he cannot yet distinguish from himself" (Anthony Wilden). ("I was perched higher than the road's highest point and flattened what is more against a rock the same colour as myself, that is grey," says Molloy.) In Lacan's theory, "for the object to be discovered by the child it must be *absent*. At the psychological level the partial object conveys the lack which creates the desire for unity from which the movement toward identification springs — since identification is itself dependent upon the discovery of difference, itself a kind of absence." ("Nothing is less like me than this patient, reasonable child" with whom, Malone says, he has time "to frolic, ashore, in the brave company I have always longed for, always searched for.") Although space does not permit extensive discussion of Lacan's theories, the relevance of these few ideas to Moran's search for the elusive Molloy, to Malone's pursuit of Sapo, and to the Unnamable's search for the invisible Mahood can at least be suggested.

For Lacan, a subject recalls or relives the "mirror stage" of his self-discovery by constructing a monologue to be overheard, as it were, by the analyst. According to Anthony Wilden, a student and translator of Lacan:

> This is the condition which makes it possible to discover the sub-ject's truth in the linear movement of his discourse. . . . Whereas linguists tend to view speech as essentially static—that is to say, as subject to the mechanics of articulation and to time in a non-essential way—Lacan views speech as a movement towards something, an attempt to fill the gaps without which speech could not be articulated. In other words, speech is as dependent upon the notion of *lack* as is the theory of desire.
>
> (*The Language of the Self*)

Although Beckett's trilogy is most certainly not *about* psychoanalysis it is possible (especially if we remember that Beckett himself underwent psychiatric therapy) to see each of his narrators as subjects attempting to unite with other selves, or objects, *by means of language alone*. Their movement toward, into, and out of each other depends upon their ability to speak and write to us as if we were Lacan's silent analyst. But unlike the subjects of psychoanalysis, Beckett's autobiographers do not merely imagine other selves; they can, within their fictional world, bring each other to life.

The other important difference between Lacan's theory and Beckett's aesthetic is that whereas for Lacan the subject is always more real than the image of the object with whom he identifies, for Beckett both identities or images are equally real: Molloy exists for us as surely as Moran, and Sapo becomes as real as Malone, at which point the two collide to create Macmann. If Sapo forced Malone to look back, to re-create his past, Macmann allows Sapo-Malone to move forward with the story in the fictive "now": Macmann lives in the new present which has emerged from the "decantation" of the future self (Malone) into the past (Sapo). "I slip into him," the narrator says in the present tense, "in the hope of learning something." And in fact, the story of Macmann seems to continue from the point at which Molloy ends his narrative:

For he did not know quite where he was, except that he was

in a plain, and the mountains not far, nor the sea, nor the town.
. . . But Macmann would have been more than human, after forty
or forty-five minutes of sanguine expectation, seeing the rain persist
as heavy as ever and day recede at last, if he had not begun to
reproach himself on what he had done, namely with having lain
down on the ground instead of continuing on his course.

Eventually, Macmann finds himself at a cell in an asylum not unlike the room
Malone had originally described as his abode. Moreover, he is cared for by
a woman who very much resembles Malone's caretaker. The latter, Malone
had said, is "even older than I. But rather less well preserved, in spite of
her mobility." Recast as Moll, this mother-figure becomes a lover, as well.
But whose lover—Macmann's or the narrator's? At times it is difficult to
know who is speaking. At one point, for example, the narrator imagines
himself "To be dead, before her, on her, with her . . . and never have to
die any more, from among the living." But later, returning to himself, he
allows "Not that, not even that." Instead, he announces, "Moll. I'm going
to kill her."

After Moll's death, and the arrival of Lemuel, Macmann's story begins
to anticipate, rather than to follow, the narrator's. Macmann asks Lemuel
questions, "but it was seldom he got an immediate answer." It is not until
after Macmann's interrogation that the narrator is visited by a similarly menac-
ing character who "may be important." Since the narrator no longer has the
use of his voice, he must write down, in the same exercise book that contains Macmann's story, a series of questions corresponding roughly to but
extending beyond those Macmann had asked Lemuel: "1. Who are you? 2.
What do you do for a living?" and so on. In this way, Lemuel becomes a link
between Macmann and his narrator. After his appearance as their common
keeper, it is impossible to know for certain which voice is narrating the story:
the narrator's, or that of his "child" Macmann. The confusion is compounded
by one last image in the birth-death cluster:

> I am being given, if I may venture the expression, birth to into
> death, such is my impression. The feet are clear already, of the
> great cunt of existence. Favorable presentation, I trust. My head
> will be the last to die. Haul in your hands. I can't. The render
> rent. My story ended I'll be living yet. Promising lag. That is
> the end of me. I shall say I no more.

Who is dying, the narrator or Macmann? And who is being born?
There are two characters dying, as Malone and his "little creature" Sapo
once died, into each other. Sentences five and six suggest that they, the nar-

rator and Macmann, are talking to each other. And from these two dying
personae, a third hybrid narrator is born, who will conclude the novel. "I
shall say 'I' no more," the old narrator says. The *new* narrator is then free
to make a fiction about this double death by equipping the sadistic Lemuel
with a weapon:

> Lemuel is in charge, he raises his hatchet on which the blood will
> never dry, but not to hit anyone . . . he will not touch anyone
> any more, either with it or with it or with it or with or with
> it or with his hammer or with his stick or with his fist or in
> thought in dream I mean never he will never or with his pencil
> or with his stick.

Lemuel kills, with his pencil-stick (stolen, perhaps from Malone), Macmann
and all of the other cell-mates, including "the Saxon" and "a young man
. . . in an old rocking chair" (Mercier and Camier?), "a small thin man"
with an umbrella (Moran?), and a "misshapen giant, bearded" (Molloy?).
But Lemuel will not kill anyone any more because he, too, is a fiction who
must die as soon as the narrator grows silent. On the page as in the story
there is "never anything any more."

Although Lemuel is the fictitious killer of his charges, the true cause
of their "deaths" would seem to be their convergence into each other. In
the small boat at sea, their bodies cease to be distinguishable, and they no
longer speak: "This tangle of grey bodies is they. Silent, dim, perhaps clinging to one another, their heads buried in their cloaks, they lie together in
a heap, in the night." This conclusion directly inverts those of earlier choral
narrations. Whereas *Absalom, Absalom!*, *Bleak House*, *Wuthering Heights*, and
other multi-vocal fictions allow pairs of complementary narrating characters
to accumulate, congregate, and conclude collectively with more authority
than we would ascribe to any single one of them, Beckett defines each of
his new narrators as the negation of the last; their "collision" creates, then,
a void, a "blessed absence." Retrospectively, we can see that each new pair
of characters has less than the last of that which most fictional (and non-
fictional) characters have in common. For example, Molloy is, as most readers
recognize, a Moran without family, property, or physical mobility. Malone
has even less of these, but he attempts to restore to himself at least a vestige
of companionship by inventing Sapo: "And if I tell of me and of that other
who is my little one, it is as always for want of love, well I'll be buggered,
I wasn't expecting that, want of a homuncule."

Ironically, however, Sapo himself suffers the loss he was meant to restore;
isolated from family and friends, he becomes Macmann who, in turn, loses

even his Moll. And this process of deprivation continues (though, as we shall see, with important modification) with the invention and destruction of Mahood and Worm, in the third volume. One might say, then, that whereas for Faulkner, Conrad, Dickens, and Brontë (among others), the search for truth about the hero or heroine is an additive process in which all narrators participate, in Beckett's trilogy it is subtractive or, in his words, "excavatory" (*Proust*). The Beckettian "author" is whoever or whatever remains after all his spokesmen have been destroyed.

As Olga Bernal brilliantly shows, the decomposition of authorial personae is accompanied by the disintegration of the trilogy's prose style and syntax. The authorial murmur speaking from within all narrators is always striving to be silent, at which point it would be paradoxically telling the truth about itself. And yet, even as Beckett's narrators die into each other, and even as their sentences dissolve, their voices paradoxically multiply, remaining "behind," as it were, in the text. Their written words cannot be erased. That is why, although the Unnamable sees circling about him only one character in whom all others reside ("To tell the truth, I believe they are all here, at least from Murphy on, but so far I have only seen Malone"), he hears more than one voice: "There are sounds here, from time to time, let that suffice. This cry to begin with, since it was the first. And others, rather different. I am getting to know them. I do not know them all." Here, the Unnamable echoes a statement made earlier by Moran about a voice he had heard "telling me things. I was getting to know it better now, to understand what it wanted." It would appear, then, that the singular voice heard by Moran becomes, in the course of the trilogy, plural, as more and more narrators invent each other. That is why, even by dying (and despite Beckett's original intentions), Malone cannot end the trilogy. For he leaves behind him his disembodied voice, which now speaks through the Unnamable, and those of his fictions, which speak *to* the Unnamable.

As the apparent creator of all earlier narrators, the Unnamable vows to succeed where Malone had failed: to conclude, by himself, the trilogy. But first, he must silence the false voices speaking through and to him: "On their own ground, with their own arms, I'll scatter them, and their miscreated puppets," he promises, adding, "it's entirely a matter of voices, no other metaphor is appropriate." To accomplish this task, the Unnamable must somehow reverse the narrative process which has made necessary the formation of this maddening chorus. But "there's no getting rid of them without naming them and their contraptions, that's the thing to keep in mind." So the Unnamable proceeds to rewrite, one last time, the story that has been twice told by his own fictions.

He begins by returning to the tale of A and C with which *Molloy* began:

> I shall tell of an incident that has only occurred once, so far. I
> await its recurrence without impatience. Two shapes, then, oblong
> like man, entered into collision before me. They fell and I saw
> them no more. I naturally thought of the pseudo-couple Mercier-
> Camier. The next time they enter the field, moving slowly toward
> each other, I shall know they are going to collide, fall and disap-
> pear, and this will enable me to see them better. Wrong. I con-
> tinue to see Malone as darkly as the first time.

If we understand that the "pseudo-couple" the Unnamable takes to be Mercier-
Camier could just as easily be Molloy-Moran (the identities of A and C having been mistaken before), it is possible to read this passage as a summary
of the first two volumes of the trilogy: in the first, Molloy (C) and Moran
(A) fall together to create Malone, and in the second, two other characters
emerge *from* Malone. Malone remains, then, the darkly visible synthesis. To
"scatter" him on his "own ground," the Unnamable resorts to Malone's own
strategy. As Malone created "companions" in Sapo and Macmann, the Unnamable will create a companion for Malone:

> He emerges as from heavy hangings, advances a few steps, looks
> at me, then backs away. He is stooping and seems to be dragging
> invisible burdens. What I see best is his hat. The crown is all
> worn through, like the sole of an old boot, giving vent to a straggle
> of grey hairs. He raises his eyes and I feel a long imploring gaze,
> as if I could do something for him. . . . His visit has never coin-
> cided, up to now, with the transit of Malone.

This creature, who is later named Mahood, bears an uncanny resemblance
to Molloy's "C." The cycle is starting again.

But this time, it seems to be going backwards. In the previous volumes,
each narrator discovered or invented an antithetical self, with whom he merged
to create a third narrator. But the Unnamable reverses that process: instead
of creating in Mahood *another* self, he ascribes to Mahood all those attributes
we had assumed were his own to begin with: "it's Mahood, this caricature
is he," we are told. "It was he told me stories about me, lived in my stead,
issued forth from me, came back to me, entered back into me, heaped stories
on my head. . . . And still today, as he would say, though he plagues me
no more his voice is there, in mine, but less, less." Thus the Unnamable
casts off his identity, rather than assuming a new one. Whatever he *was*,
Mahood *is*.

To put it another way, Mahood is to the Unnamable what Sapo was to Malone: a past self. But whereas Malone was the inventor of Sapo's life, it is Mahood who supplies the Unnamable with memories of a bizarre childhood: "That's one of Mahood's favorite tricks, to produce ostensibly independent testimony in support of my historical existence." The plot, too, is reversed. Whereas Sapo leaves his family (as well as the Lamberts), the Unnamable attempts to return to his. But "According to Mahood, I never reached them, that is to say they all died first, the whole ten or eleven of them, carried off by sausage poisoning." Malone had been unable to distinguish his fictions from his life. But the Unnamable knows that Mahood is feeding him lies about a family he never had: "his voice continued to testify for me, as though woven into mine, preventing me from saying who I was, what I was, so as to have done with saying, done with listening." If the Unnamable is to speak the truth (that is, paradoxically, to become silent), Mahood must first be quieted.

The Unnamable attempts to rid himself of Mahood as Malone had "lost" Sapo—by inventing another, future persona. As Macmann replaced Sapo, Worm is meant to supercede Mahood: "Worm. . . . It will be my name too, when the time comes, when I needn't be called Mahood any more." Now if Worm were merely an older Mahood (as Molloy seems to be an older Moran, and Macmann an older Sapo) we might expect them to unite in the creation of yet another "author," yet another volume. But in an effort to end this cycle or spiral, the Unnamable alters the pattern: "Before Mahood there were others like him, of the same breed and creed, armed with the same prong. But Worm is the first of his kind." What the others have lost, Worm never had: property, history, arms, legs. But more importantly, he lacks what every other character has: ability to speak or write. "I have not ceased to hear his murmur all the while the others discoursed," the Unnamable says. But "Worm cannot note." Theoretically, then, just as Moran's coalescence with Molloy entails the loss of the former's property, the convergence of Mahood, Worm and the Unnamable should result in silence. In reality, however, the strategy fails. For, as the Unnamable slowly realizes, he can invent Worm, but he cannot really become Worm—or at least, he cannot tell us if he has: "I'm Worm, no, if I were Worm I wouldn't know it, I wouldn't say it, I'd be Worm." And he wonders, if "when I have failed to be Worm I'll be Mahood, automatically, on the rebound?"

Having finally realized that the story of "A" and "C," those two objectified selves, can never be ended, the Unnamable resorts to one last modification of its bipolar form. Instead of naming two antithetical personae, he divides himself into two unnamed pronominal persons—"I" and "he"—yet he refuses to become either one:

I'll have said it inside me, then in the same breath outside me, perhaps that's what I feel, an outside and an inside and me in the middle, perhaps that's what I am, the thing that divides the world in two, on the one side the outside, on the other the inside, that can be as thin as foil, I'm neither one side nor the other, I'm in the middle, I'm the partition, I've two surfaces and no thickness, perhaps that's what I feel, myself vibrating, I'm the tympanum, on the one hand the mind, on the other the world.

Thus he suspends himself both grammatically and dramatically between subject and object, perceiver and perceived, teller and listener. This brilliant maneuver allows him (the singular pronoun is misleading) to slip out of, rather than into, whichever self is speaking: "I seem to speak, that's because he says I as if he were I, I nearly believed him, do you hear him." By means of this grammatical inversion, the Unnamable forces us to think of him not as an "I" but as a "he," the silent, unnamable yet true hero of the trilogy. "I'll go on," a voice says repeatedly. But "he" imposes silence, and the novel finally ends.

In one sense, the apparent assimilation of all other narrating characters by the Unnamable "author" may be seen to follow formal convention set by earlier multi-vocal fictions. The narrators of *Lord Jim* and *Absalom, Absalom!*, for example, become authorial and achieve closure by repeating or transcribing the words of collaborating characters. But in Beckett's fiction, narrating characters do not merely collaborate; they coalesce. At the beginning of *The Unnamable*, all of the "author's" paired personae have dissolved into a single narrating mind that speaks "no words but the words of others." It is this mind, in fact, that has created the narrative chorus, being "sufficiently impressed by certain expressions to make a vow, while continuing my yelps, never to forget them, and, what is more, to ensure they should engender others." But the Unnamable also knows that, while allowing these "others" to speak, he himself has been forced to tell lies. "All these Murphys, Molloys and Malones do not fool me," he claims. "They have made me waste my time, suffer for nothing, speak of them when, in order to stop speaking, I should have spoken of me and of me alone." Therefore, he not only rewrites, but in effect unwrites their stories, reversing their narrative strategies so as to become silent. In earlier choral narrations, the "real" heroes and heroines emerge for the reader only after all voices have spoken. But in Beckett's trilogy, the truth does not follow immediately from the formation of a narrative chorus, but rather resides in the silence following its self-destruction. In three separate yet mutually dependent texts, Beckett takes the art of multi-vocal fiction to the very limit of language itself.

Naming the M/inotaur:
Beckett's Trilogy and the Failure
of Narrative

Roch C. Smith

Speaking of the labyrinth in *La Terre et les rêveries du repos*, Gaston Bachelard reiterates his fundamental view that, in a dream, the roles of subject and object are inverted. For the dreamer, what appears to be objective reality never precedes the subjective state but is, instead, shaped by that state. According to Bachelard,

> it is not because *the passage is narrow* that the dreamer is *com-pressed*—it is because the dreamer is *anguished* that he sees the road *get narrower*. . . . Thus, in a dream, the labyrinth is neither seen nor foreseen, it is not presented as a perspective of roads. It must be lived to be seen. The contortions of the dreamer, his contorted movements within the material of the dream leave *a labyrinth in their wake*. . . . Ariadne's thread is a thread of discourse. It belongs to the narrated dream. It is a thread of return.

More recently, J. Hillis Miller has offered a similar comparison of Ariadne's thread to what he calls "repetition" of the narrative line—that is, "anything which happens to the line to trouble or even to confound its straightforward linearity: returnings, knottings, recrossings, crinklings to and fro, suspensions, interruptions, fictionalizings" ("Ariadne's Thread: Repetition and Narrative Line"). Also like Bachelard, Miller considers that the objective correlative to the subject's vision emerges only after the narrative thread of return has been completely woven. The beast (Bachelard's "object") is not the cause of the chase; rather, the chase (Bachelard's "subject") brings about the beast.

From *Modern Fiction Studies* 29, no. 1 (Spring 1983). © 1983 by the Purdue Research Foundation, West Lafayette, Indiana.

"The chase has a beast in view. The end of the story is the retrospective revelation of the law of the whole. That law is an underlying 'truth' which ties all together in an inevitable sequence revealing a hitherto hidden figure in the carpet" (Miller).

Richard Macksey has seen the dissolution of character in Beckett's trilogy as an imprisonment of the self within a labyrinth. And certainly Miller's definition of narrative repetition seems made to order as a description of the trilogy with its labyrinthine twists, turns, and interruptions. Moreover, in accord with both Bachelard's and Miller's views, Beckett's novelistic labyrinth does not preexist the narration itself. It is not mimetic; rather, it appears as the result of the narrative process. It is the wake left by Molloy turning out his pages, Moran writing his report, Malone weaving his tales and taking inventory, and the unnamable narrator, whether "I," "he," or Worm, leaving a silky trail, a spider's web of narrative confusion.

Initially, of course, there are stories of physical wandering, particularly with Molloy, whom Ruby Cohn has called the "archetype of the fabulous voyager." And, as the trilogy's narrative is played out, motion that was thought to be linear turns out to be circular. Molloy is forced "to go in a circle, hoping in this way to go in a straight line"; Moran carefully paces in a circle as he waits for his son to return from Hole with a bicycle; and Macmann, rolling upon the ground, discovers that he was advancing "along the arc of a gigantic circle." In *The Unnamable* the narrator's physical wandering has ceased, but we find the narration itself emanating from a sphere—variously described as "an egg" and "a big talking ball"—whose goal, as expressed through the narrator's surrogate, Mahood, is to go on "not always in a straight line," first a prisoner in a "circular" building, then on the island he says he never left and where, he tells us, "I wind my endless ways."

Yet the perambulation is not only circular; it is increasingly cloistered as the rambler finds himself inside dark enclosed places as small as a "head" (*MD*) or "my distant skull where once I wandered" (*U*), till he can wander no more. He is caught in an inescapable web of words where

> to go on means going from here, means finding me, losing me, vanishing and beginning again, a stranger first, then little by little the same as always, in another place, where I shall say I have always been, of which I shall know nothing, being incapable of seeing, moving, thinking, speaking, but of which little by little, in spite of these handicaps, I shall begin to know something, just enough for it to turn out to be the same place as always.
>
> (*The Unnamable*)

For the entire trilogy moves toward a gradual replacement of physical wandering, first with the narrator's fictional accounts of the wandering of others and finally with the purely verbal narrative wandering we find in *The Unnamable*, where to "go on" is to write, to produce more words. The narrator's increasingly frequent reminders that he is, and was, telling stories culminate, in *The Unnamable*, in a reduction of all fiction, including earlier tales of wandering, to the words that make it up. Bicycles, crutches, chamberpots, sticks, hats, and jars, even the characters themselves are, after all, but words: "I'm in words, made of words, others' words, what others, the place too, the air, the walls, the floor, the ceiling, all words." Words overcome the object they were seemingly meant to represent as the stories get tangled in their own verbal web.

Molloy's description of a small silver object made of two crosses joined by a bar serves as a particularly graphic example of this process. The description seems much more detailed than such an innocuous object deserves, especially because, despite all this attention, the object is never identified. Molloy indicates that

> the crosses [X's in the original French] of the little object I am referring to were perfect, that is to say composed each of two identical V's, one upper with its opening above, like all V's for that matter, and the other lower with its opening below, or more precisely of four rigorously identical V's the two I have just named and then two more, one on the right hand, the other on the left, having their openings on the right and left respectively. But perhaps it is out of place to speak here of right and left, of upper and lower.

Molloy further describes this unnamed object as a "strange instrument" for which he says he felt "affection" and even "veneration." Moreover, he explains that he "could never understand what possible purpose it could serve," although he did not doubt "that it had a most specific function always to be hidden from me."

Because we know that Molloy took the object from Lousse's house along with coffee spoons and other silverware, we may well assume that it is nothing more than a kniferest. Such a conjecture is reinforced by the fact that the narrator in *Malone Dies* makes a specific reference to "a little silver kniferest" as the only object of value found in Macmann's pockets. And we know how things have a tendency to reappear from story to story throughout the trilogy. But if we return to Molloy's description, we note that, although it may leave us unsatisfied about the physical identity of the object, it leaves absolutely no doubt about its verbal properties. The object is made of connected letters—

X's and V's—and is therefore a *word* at least as much as it is a kniferest. That explains why Molloy, as would any writer, feels affection and veneration for this precious object whose function is both precise and obscure.

The silver kniferest, then, is what Jean Ricardou has called a "structural metaphor" (*Problèmes du nouveau roman*) in that it is both an object within the story and an image of the writer's own text. In *Malone Dies* the words themselves, like Macmann's kniferest, are all the narrator has of value. In *Molloy* the symmetrical object-word parallels the rough symmetry of the novel. Its X's and V's like crossroads in the labyrinth offer no guidance as to the correct direction one should take. For in a narrative, Miller reminds us, "any single thread leads everywhere, like a labyrinth made of a single line or corridor crinkled to and fro." Significantly, Miller gives as an example of this phenomenon "the letter X. . . . a letter, a sign, but a sign for signs generally." Thus the silver kniferest metaphorically summarizes the view implicit in the trilogy that language no longer is an instrument of representation but, as Olga Bernal has expressed it, "the very matter with which literature is at grips." Beckett's maze is a textual one beyond which there is literally "nothing," not even suffering, as the disembodied narrator of *The Unnamable* reminds us when he refers to this "Labyrinthine torment that can't be grasped, or limited, or felt, or suffered, no not even suffered." In attempting to "unravel his tangle," the narrator must follow the maze of words he himself has woven.

Like Theseus, he seeks out the beast hidden somewhere in the loops and twists of this labyrinth. Yet, because the maze is verbal, the monster must be slain with words; it must be *named* if it is to stop exacting its tribute of words from the hapless narrator. The names multiply to the point that there seem to be many such monsters, yet "there's no getting rid of them without naming them." This is the fundamental dilemma facing the narrator lost in an increasingly complicated labyrinth of unstoppable words. He can't go on adding more words and increasing the complexity of his narrative labyrinth, yet he must go on because the only way out is through words, or so it seems. So he follows his own exhortation to "weave, weave." Like a spider in the middle of his web he continues spinning in order to find the word that would end the succession of puppets—the Molloys, Molloses, Morans, Marthas, Macmanns, Molls, Mahoods, Matthews, Marguerites, Madeleines, their predecessors and variants, the Murphys, Watts, Merciers, Worms, and Lemuels, not to mention the mothers and Mags—who people the spirals of his prose with its most striking repetition, the letter M, the M/inotaur of his verbal labyrinth.

For it is part of the narrator's dilemma throughout the trilogy that he is at once the hunter and the hunted, the weaver of the labyrinth and the beast it encloses, Ariadne and Theseus, as well as the unnamable M/inotaur. Like Daedalus, he is caught in the coils of his own creation, a fate shared with many modern artists, as Richard Macksey points out. But it is much worse for Beckett's narrator because, unlike his Athenean forbear, he cannot find a means of escape, and all attempts to do so entangle him further in his verbal prison. The enemy is within, so the narrator must be both executioner and victim. Thus Molloy searches for his mother and finds *himself*; Moran searches for Molloy and ends by uncannily resembling the object of his search to the point that Moran is "devoured" by Molloy, as Ruby Cohn so aptly observed. Later Macmann slowly takes on the characteristics of Malone, including his paralysis and even his hat, whereas Malone, passing silently before the narrator of *The Unnamable*, might be taken for "Molloy wearing Malone's hat."

None of the trilogy's narrators is able to find an escape from this web of words. Theirs is a narrative doomed to failure. The M/inotaur, even when stripped of his fictional disguises, is forever out of reach, and silence, the only true escape from a labyrinth of words, is therefore impossible, as we see in the following passage from *The Unnamable*:

> But now, is it now, I on me? Sometimes I think it is. And then I realize it is not. I am doing my best, and failing again, yet again. I don't mind failing, it's a pleasure, but I want to go silent.

How widespread is this pleasurable failure? And what is its role in Beckett's trilogy? The narrator fails, of course, to create a fiction that will reveal the truth about his elusive beast and allow him to go silent. But already Moran, whose wanderings mirror the labyrinthine thread of narration, wonders, when his leg begins to slow him down, if he is not "secretly glad that this had happened to me, perhaps even to the point of not wanting to get well?" And Malone, painfully aware of the failure of his fiction to invent, to name the M/inotaur, rails at "How false all this is. No time now to explain. I began again, no longer in order to succeed, but in order to fail." Finally, in *The Unnamable*, the narrator expresses his frustration at the paradox of writing: "What can it matter to me that I succeed or fail? The undertaking is none of mine, if they want me to succeed I'll fail, and vice versa, so as not to be rid of my tormentors." The point, one that is not fully realized until *The Unnamable*, is that fiction must fail as "storytelling" if it is to have any hope of succeeding as "naming." The narration of fiction, the weaving of a verbal tapestry, multiplies words and carries the narrator further away from the exit of his verbal labyrinth and from the silence he seeks. It is this realization that is behind the gradual disappearance of storytelling as one moves from *Molloy* to *The Unnamable*.

But what replaces the narration of fiction? Here we do well to return to Jean Ricardou, whose theoretical reversal of these two terms—narration and fiction—matches Beckett's practice in the trilogy and provides a means of articulating our experience as readers of these works. For Ricardou, a "new novel" such as Robbe-Grillet's *Project for a Revolution in New York* is marked by a fiction that "emanates from the narrative process and contributes in some way to describing it. Fiction is, most often, a fiction of narration." In such works it is not a question of telling a story about the activities of revolutionaries in New York, for instance, but of telling the story of telling such a story, thereby revealing more about the narrative process than about the story itself. As Ricardou explains, "the novel ceases to be the writing of a story in order to become the story of a writing." Such a novel is deliberately aware of its own workings; it is quite literally "self-conscious." This is particularly true of Beckett's novels where, as Dieter Wellershoff put it, "literature has reached a point at which it is looking over its own shoulders."

The Unnamable is, of course, replete with the stops, twists, and convolutions of the self-conscious novel as the narrator hesitates between the stories of Mahood, Worm, "I," and "he." But pervasive as it is in the last novel of the trilogy, such expressed awareness of the conventions of writing fiction is already a part of earlier works, as *Molloy* makes clear:

> And every time I say, I said this, or I said that, or speak of a voice saying, far away inside of me, Molloy, and then a fine phrase more or less clear and simple, or find myself compelled to attribute to others intelligible words, or hear my own voice uttering to others more or less articulate sounds, I am merely complying with the convention that demands you either lie or hold your peace.

The ubiquitous voice, which in *Molloy* and *Malone Dies* begins as an inner murmur or buzzing before turning out intelligible words and whose compulsive power energizes *The Unnamable*, is the voice of narration stripped of its usual fictional baffles by the fiction of narration.

Yet even thus exposed, the fiction of narration does not succeed. Beckett's narrator does not seek merely to bare the word; he seeks to stop it. His goal is not to create novel fictional forms but to still the voice of fiction in order to say "nothing." But, as the narrator of *The Unnamable* ruefully points out, "it seems impossible to speak and yet say nothing, you think you have succeeded, but you always overlook something, a little yes, a little no, enough to exterminate a regiment of dragoons." It is a task at which he must inevitably fail because it is literally not possible to "say nothing," to express what the narrator of *The Unnamable* calls "the unthinkable unspeakable." As the narrator resignedly asks near the end of that novel, "how can I say it, that's all words, they're all I have and not many of them, the words fail, the voice fails, so be it." For, unlike the work of a new novelist like Robbe-Grillet, Beckett's is not merely a fiction of narration but a *fiction of failed narrative*. The trilogy reflects Beckett's view, expressed to Georges Duthuit, "that to be an artist is to fail, as no other dare fail, that failure is his world and the shrink from it desertion."

Yet, if the trilogy is the story of the narrator's growing awareness of the narrative dilemma, it is also the expression of a fundamental paradox because it is failure itself that makes possible the continuation of narrative, tenuous as that continuation may be. The narrative circularity of *Molloy* is only apparently closed; Malone's pencil lead grows perilously short, but it never runs out; and the "unthinkable unspeakable" may be unnamable, but the narrative thread goes on. The narrator of *The Unnamable* summarizes this paradox when he insists that "the search for a means to put an end to things, an end to speech, is what enables discourse to continue." Increasingly, the narrator weaves the story of the impossibility of expression, but he does not stop weaving. Whatever hope Beckett's trilogy offers would seem to be found in this unbroken narrative line whose tensile strength barely resists, yet does not break, despite the tugs and pulls of despair. A modern-day Scheherazade, Beckett keeps hope alive solely by telling stories of failed narrative whose nights in "Ballybaba" and "the fresh air of Turdybaba" (*M*) ironically echo the traditional storytelling of the *Arabian Nights* and serve as reminders of the transformation of fiction into a labyrinthine quest for silence.

Beckett's narrator lives in what Bachelard, in another context, called a "logosphere" or "universe of the word," yet, like Derrida, the narrator is wary of a "logocentrism which is also a phonocentrism: an absolute proximity of voice and being" (*Of Grammatology*). For Moran it seems that "all language was an excess of language," and Malone reluctantly resigns himself to the notion that his life is reduced to a "child's exercise book," whereas the narrator of *The Unnamable* remarks that

> it has not yet been our good fortune to establish with any degree of accuracy what I am, where I am, whether I am words among words, or silence in the midst of silence, to recall only two of the hypotheses launched in this connexion, though silence to tell the truth does not appear to have been very conspicuous up to now, but appearances may sometimes be deceptive.

Thus compelled to utter words, for that is all he has, but uncertain about whether such words have an ontological significance, the narrator will go on. Yet because the ontological question remains unresolved, no fixed figure ever appears in the carpet. Despite it all, or, rather, because of it all, the difficult weaving continues in this fiction of failed narrative that can only exist in the tortuous and tenuous space between logos and silence.

The Harpooned Notebook: *Malone Dies*

H. Porter Abbott

I wish to focus on how Samuel Beckett's *Malone Dies* carries on one of the traditional modes of the novel: the intercalated or nonretrospective narrative. In what I am calling a mode, I mean to include that abundance of novels in letter or diary form which have been produced from the earliest years of the novel, which are still with us, and which require at least two principal fictions: that the narrative we read is written by at least one of its principal characters and that the time of its writing is contained by the time of the events recorded. *Malone* is the extremest example of the mode I know. So extreme is it that one is tempted to call it a travesty or grotesque satire. My argument is that it is in fact, in its extremity, not satire but a continuation of the mode, carried out in much the same spirit as that of its early practitioners. To tackle this, I must first reduce the field. There is an array of conventions, or *topoi*, that recur in a sort of loose confederation through the history of this mode, many of which can be found, faintly or vividly, in *Malone*. In my argument, I shall focus on three: two central and one peripheral. They are, respectively, the threatened manuscript, the merging of the times of narrative and narration, and the blank entry.

The *topos*, or motif, of the threatened manuscript gives us a good place to start because it bears directly on the crucial documentary character of the mode. It will allow me to expand a bit here at the beginning on the traditional importance, in this mode, of the text as a material object or empirical certainty. In studies of the eighteenth-century novel, this importance has generally been accounted for by its appeal to a conception of reality biased—by

From *Samuel Beckett: Humanistic Perspectives*, edited by Morris Beja, S. E. Gontarski, and Pierre Astier. © 1983 by Ohio State University Press.

science and middle-class attitudes—toward the material and the measurable. Thus an art form came of age disguised as a form of nonart. It pretended not only to tell "true" stories in the words of "real" people (as opposed to professional authors), but also to provide the objective evidence of these stories in the form of letters or diaries that often comprised in themselves the whole of the narration.

But if this emphasis on the physical text had its roots in a bourgeois or vulgarly scientific fixation on the visible and the material, one of its major consistent functions was to give testimony to the invisible and nonmaterial. In a paradox that is perhaps more verbal than real, the text's degree of materiality and visible exactitude constituted its credentials as a testimony of the spirit. In the eighteenth century, this was particularly true of those novels that came out of a Puritan or sentimental frame of mind. When Pamela asks permission to rewrite one of her letters before turning it over to Mr. B., he protests that she must leave it exactly as it is "because," he tells her, "they are your true sentiments at *the time*, and because they were *not* written for my perusal." The letters are an archeological record of precisely how what we cannot see in Pamela—that is, what is really important about Pamela—moved at the time. And as we read them, our invisible natures are moved too. Not to be so moved is to miss their significance—that is, to be hopelessly materialistic.

So what is curious is the combination. The spirit cannot be taken for granted. Correlatively, a story cannot be just a story. A material artifact is required as evidence of a particular spirit. As the time of her certain departure from this world draws near, Clarissa takes great pains to ensure the perpetuation of her letters—the literary evidence of her existence—in their exact form. The urgency of her concern is an odd element in the story of her life, considering her avowed confidence in the universe, how it is constituted, by Whom and to what end. So it is possible that her concern for the texts of her letters in this material world expresses her—and no doubt her author's—submerged uncertainty about the invisible world.

Readers shared Clarissa's anxiety about the physical preservation of the manuscript, and for this reason threats to the existence of the document became standard equipment of the mode I am discussing. Manuscripts have been scorched and water-soaked, rescued from fire, mildewed, eaten by worms, stuffed in boxes, lost, buried, bottled and floated upon the sea. When the diaries of Lermontov's Pechorin are flung upon the ground in anger, one after the other, it goes to the heart. The drama of the survival of the text has become a part of the drama of the tale. Frequently augmenting this drama is the fact that the diarist or letter-writer is dead by the time we read the evidence of his or her life. The text is all that remains. Moreover, a good many of the writers are not only dead as we read but doomed or dying even as they write.

This is the tradition that Malone dies into. In the context of Beckett's literary career, *Malone Dies* comes at that point when Beckett, moving closer and closer to the page, suddenly brought the document itself into focus before plunging on through it into the "Where now? Who now? When now?" of the monologue that follows. At the point of focus, Beckett brings the whole tradition of which I have been speaking into focus at the same time—but seen now, as it were, so close up that it appears a grotesque caricature. Never has there been so wasted a moribund. Rarely has the room in which he writes been so thoroughly an enclosure, so thoroughly an expression of his isolation. And rarely has the document itself been so continually at risk. Its existence depends not on a pen but on a pencil—and one so used that its life is barely that of the writer. Sharpened at both ends, it is reduced by the last pages to a small piece of lead. As for the exercise-book, it gets lost, falls on the floor, at one point is "harpooned" by Malone with his stick.

By such means does Beckett augment the metaphysical anxiety—for so long a part of the mode—that drives reader and writer alike to want to hold fast to the material document. This anxiety is also brilliantly augmented by Beckett's inclusion of a distinct remnant of the novel's middle-class origins: the inventory of his goods and chattels that Malone is so concerned to make. In evoking this annual rite of shopkeepers, here hopelessly botched, Beckett goes beyond satire to the heart of the businessman's very human ailment. You cannot take it with you. Moreover, once he is fully launched on his enterprise, Malone finds that by his definition (those things are his he can lay hold of) "nothing is mine anymore . . . except my exercise-book, my lead and the French pencil, assuming it really exists." Now the French pencil, he cannot lay his hands on. And the lead is doomed. This leaves only one possession, as he has anticipated: "No, nothing of all that is mine. But the exercise-book is mine, I can't explain." Malone's text is his only thing.

In *Malone Dies*, the whole business of possessions and inventories, of the entire material universe, draws to a point. Malone, at the end of this history, resigns himself to the suppressed intuition that led Clarissa to expend so much energy on the fate of her letters. "This exercise-book is my life," he says at last, "this child's exercise-book, it has taken me a long time to resign myself to that." But in resigning himself, Malone at the same time relinquishes both the book and the "life." In coalescing words with things, Beckett puts them on one side of a gulf, on the other side of which Malone maintains his allegiance, however reluctantly, to the wordless and immaterial.

In this Malone shows a deeper conviction of the invisible than Clarissa, and a deeper commitment to it, just as his creator exposes the book and its words as a snare and a delusion—not the right vehicle after all. The skewered notebook brings to an end the tradition of meticulous fictional editing that begins with Richardson.

The next element that I wish to discuss is the tendency of nonretrospective art to close the gap between the time of the narrating and the time of the narrated, of *discours* and *histoire*. To put this in other words, the narrative in this mode aspires to the warmest possible relationship to time. Early intimations of this can be seen in Milton's expansion of the conventional epic invocation of the muse to a periodic reunion with time in which he expands on what Malone would call his "present state." This aesthetic merging with time is essentially what Beckett focused on in his valuation of Proust as a romantic. The classical artist, by contrast, "raises himself artificially out of Time in order to give relief to his chronology and causality to his development." From this point of view, the dying Malone, whose time finally runs out, is the ultimate romantic artist; and his exercise-book, the final collapse of art into time.

What is missing in Malone and what is essential to many of his romantic predecessors is a belief that form and time are compatible: moreover, that genuine form (as opposed to artificial, classical form) can be tapped by merging with time. It is a theory that runs parallel to the theory of spontaneous artistic creation and resides in a faith that form is an aspect of the invisible. Goethe's Werther was guided by it in his effusions. Later, Coleridge, drawing on the ideas of Schlegel, called such form "organic" and opposed it to "mechanic" or imposed form. In his Conversation Poems, which are a species of diaristic moments, Coleridge sought to submit himself to this vital forming agency by submitting himself to time. Tennyson sought the same thing in his long poetic diary *In Memoriam*. As Tennyson points out in the poem itself, it was only through his submission to time that he achieved the form of *In Memoriam*, a form in the shape of a curve extending from grief to rejoicing.

The difference between Malone and his romantic predecessors is that for Malone form and time are completely at odds. This dissociation, of course, is not new with Malone. During the evolution of intercalated narrative, one can find it implicitly or explicitly in a number of late-nineteenth-century French and Scandinavian diary novels, many of them inspired by the intimate journals of Amiel. The most baldly explicit expression of the dissociation of form and time was developed by Sartre in his diary novel of 1938, *Nausea*. The difference between Malone and these later representatives of the tradition is that Malone maintains attention on the invisible, both as a mystery and as a kind of presence. Moreover, though one of his terms for the invisible is now "formlessness," he carries over from his romantic precursors their awed regard for it. It is the source of seriousness and gravity. If it is the opposite of Milton's informing Spirit, Malone employs a very Miltonic intensity, echoing the fall of Satan, in expressing his devotion to

> darkness, to nothingness, to earnestness, to home, to him waiting for me always, who needed me and whom I needed, who took me in his arms and told me to stay with him always, who gave me his place and watched over me, who suffered every time I left him, whom I have often made suffer and seldom contented, whom I have never seen.

So, again, as in the case of the threatened manuscript, Beckett maintains our attention on the absent subject by accentuating a traditional element of intercalated narrative. He compounds the collapse of mechanic form by having Malone aspire hopelessly to the condition of the omniscient and omnipotent artist. Malone draws on what remains of the left lobe of his brain to fulfill the requirements of a plan, a plan that, as we know, not only falls in ruins but begins to break down the moment it is formulated. His stories are swamped by his present state; time lies heavy on the notebook. It does so because Malone cannot help but keep faith, more even than his romantic forebears, with the invisible power, shrouded in darkness, that is the source of his vitality — "the nourishing murk," as he calls it, "that is killing me."

The final convention I wish to consider is what could be called the Blank Entry. It is a more infrequent element than the two I have discussed already, one strictly limited to the diary strain of intercalated narrative. In the blank entry, one finds the date, followed by a blank, or a question mark or, at most, some verbal formula for blankness: "Nothing at all to report today." Its close relative is the Boring Entry, which could be any such desultory non-comment as "Ate at 7:00, fell asleep shortly thereafter." They are what can make the reading of real diaries such a low-yield, searingly tedious activity. Duhamel parodied both devices in *Salavin's Journal* when he had Salavin decide to become a saint. Salavin buys a new journal, which he begins with great anticipation:

> On with the new life! Would that I were older by one year, to be able to re-read this journal and weep with joy! I am ready. I'm waiting. I'm off to meet myself.
> January 8 — Nothing to report.
> January 9 — Nothing to report.

January 10—Nothing.
January 11—Nothing that has to do with the situation in any way.
January 12—Nothing.
January 13—Nothing. It's snowing, but that's of no importance.
(To be struck out if I copy this journal.)
January 14—Nothing.

And so on for another fourteen entries. In *Nausea* Sartre parodied the same device when he had Roquentin make the entry, "Nothing. Existed," which was especially coy, since Roquentin had just achieved insights into the linked nature of both Nothingness and Existence.

In fictional diaries, the blank or boring entry is an obvious liability, one that is rarely indulged in with any frequency. Its principal function is one that it shares with a number of those devices that Ian Watt collected under the heading Formal Realism. It is a way of saying, "This is not art" (assuming the logic that if this were art, there would not be this kind of wasted space). It increases the documentary illusion. But the matter is not quite as simple as this because inevitably we cannot help knowing that this *is* art and therefore necessarily concentrated, full of import. So the blank or boring entry is also a way of saying, "Watch out, something must be preparing itself." The ratio of these two opposed functions would appear to depend on just how firmly we believe that, despite the nonretrospective appearance of the document, there is a secret teleology at work. Roquentin's comment about the traditional fat of the retrospective story is apt even for the nonretrospective document: "It was night, the street was deserted." As he says, we do not let these words pass unnoticed. We read them as annunciations of adventure, endowed with meaning by the future that preexists them. Nonretrospective structure can at once increase the legitimacy of such dullness as it increases the excitement.

Malone Dies is, in effect, an extension of the principle of the boring entry to the entire novel. It is one of the few books in which the teleological illusion Roquentin writes of, which redeems an entry of its tedium, appears to be convincingly demolished from the start. The only conclusion, a foregone one, is the writer's death, which, in the case of Malone, is basically a matter of being "quite dead at last." It is an arbitrary, radically unclimactic terminus for the words he writes. Its onset is marked by one of the blankest of blank entries:

never anything

there

any more

The only thing blanker is the blankness of the page that one may project from the last word to infinity.

But the actual blankness of the page is, in fact, something that plays a significant role in the body of this text. It pierces the text at points throughout—a whiteness separating blocks of prose. And it figures, if I am right, as the ultimate logical development, not only of the device of the blank entry, but of the mode in which I am locating the book. And it expresses in its blankness the same double quality I have been discussing, for it implies at once nothing and something that exceeds the importance of the text it sets off. There are modern examples one can find of an approach to this extreme. (I am thinking particularly of such works as Max Frisch's *I'm Not Stiller,* Doris Lessing's *The Golden Notebook*, and Alberto Moravia's *The Lie*, all of them a part of the notebook tradition and all of them, in their individual ways, inviting us to look through the falsehood of words to an invisible and inexpressible internal reality.) But I can think of few that, in the manner of *Malone Dies*, actually incorporate the total blank as a recurring element in the text—an element that operates, if you will, as a signifier.

"My notes," writes Malone, "have a curious tendency . . . to annihilate all they purport to record." But in the blanks, "the noises begin again . . . those whose turn it is." In one forty-eight-hour blank, he claims that the whole "unutterable" business of Malone and the other was brought to a "solution and conclusion." These blanks are, in effect, the ultimate means of humbling the text. They are where the action is. They signify a presence not completely unlike that for which Derrida took Rousseau to task. In the very violence Beckett exerts against the text, here in the last outpost of the notebook tradition, he preserves not only the idea but the urgency of the text's referential function.

In reviewing these three conventions—the threatened manuscript, the merging of the times of narrating and narrative, and the blank entry—I find that my humanistic perspective on Beckett has acquired a distinctly romantic coloration. I have tried to show how he writes not simply in the mode if intercalated fiction but in the spirit of its early development. In bringing each of these elements to an extreme, Beckett is perhaps the last romantic, asserting his artistic allegiance to what is invisible and mysterious and forever beyond the text.

Grammatical Insincerity
in *The Unnamable*

Edouard Morot-Sir

Samuel Beckett is not a philosopher; he never pretended to be taken for one. Nor is he a writer who wraps up philosophical ideas in literary clothes, be they poetic, dramatic, or narrative. Allegory and symbols are not his way of referring either to himself or to somebody else. He is not an artist who likes to test himself with different instruments, i.e., with varied linguistic possibilities in the accepted genres, as most of the writers of the twentieth century have done. He is fundamentally a poet who looks for the unique and rare meeting where words become at the same time music, meaning, and reference. However, Beckett the poet has always been repressed, wounded, not only, as poets usually like to be, by life, but by language itself: thus, in his works, an obsessive and sarcastic scepticism, an obstinate, desperate will not be seduced by the poetic gift or by any other gift in the manipulation of language, an anguishing quest for an impossible *linguistic sincerity*. That tension, which dramatizes Beckett's texts, from the first poems to the last ones (and I call "poem" any Beckettian text—novels and plays being nothing less than indirect and frustrated poetry), I propose to qualify it as *nonexpressionism*. It implies an ethics, a logic, and an aesthetic in reverse. It destroys ideologies at the level of social or class justification, and their deeper sources. When Beckett says in *The Unnamable* [*Un*] "Overcome, that goes without saying, the fatal leaning toward expressiveness," he denounces grammar and syntax as well as rhetoric—the logical as well as the literary devices that have dominated literatures for centuries. To be sincere, efficient—and it should

From *Writing in a Modern Temper: Essays on French Literature and Thought in Honor of Henri Peyre* (Stanford French and Italian Studies 3), edited by Mary Ann Caws. © 1984 by ANMA Libri & Co.

be more than a pious wish or a dramatic presentation which denies itself by its very success—nonexpressionism needs to become a permanent, trying fight against the traditional rhetoric ornaments, surely; but, more seriously, against the universal functions of linguistic referentiality, which are *description, naming*, especially pronominal naming, and *narration*. My enumeration follows the order suggested by Beckett at the beginning of *The Unnamable*: "Where now? Who now? When now?" (It should be noted that the French text which came before the English translation inverts the second and third questions: "Où maintenant? Quand maintenant? Qui maintenant?" This difference between the French and English versions opens the way to infinite commentaries. If the interpretation suggested in my analysis is correct, the change in order for second and third questions means that in the French order chosen first, Beckett respected the usual philosophical order of critical philosophy since David Hume and Kant, whose epistemologies go from Space to Time, from Time to Subjectivity. Working on his translation from the French to English it is possible that Beckett became more aware of the problems of writing proper, hidden behind the three philosophical questions. This could be the reason why the English text goes from description to nomination, and finally to narration, i.e., from the possibility of finding a place to the possibility of designating a person and, from there, to the possibilities of telling stories, or, in other words, to the justification of writing.)

Willy-nilly the poet finds himself at the heart of the most difficult questions of modern philosophy. What is more philosophical indeed than the problems of Space, of the Self, of Time? Descartes and Locke, Hume, Kant, Schopenhauer, and many others, made of these interrogations the very center of their epistemologies. However, in spite of numerous references to philosophers, Samuel Beckett never relied on any kind of philosophical language. He has looked and still is looking for a poetic, nonexpressionist solution for such theoretical aporias. For instance, the conclusion of the search made by *Un* reaches a recognized culmination for nonexpression that was to be succeeded by thirty years of poetic experiments. Are the first sentences of one of the recent "experiences," *Company*, not a direct echo of *Un*? "A voice comes to one in the dark. Imagine." In their double, constative and performative, assertive and exclamative way, these words give an answer to the triple enigma of *Un*. Beckettian nonexpressionism was thus dominated by the problematic of writing quartered into directions that lead to fights for three *rhetorical rights*: the *right of describing*, which corresponds to the philosophical discussions on the existence and essence of Space; the *right of the subject* or, more specifically, the right of using first person pronouns (it is well known that the subject-object relation has become, since Descartes, the modern problem of consciousness and the unconscious); finally, the *right of discursing*, that is, the double right to produce arguments and to tell stories: philosophers have transposed them into the complementary topics of reason and memory. As it appears in *Un*, the defense of those rights—a sort of chart of the writer—leads to the awareness of paradoxical values that ultimately defies any kind of writing and its legitimacy. I propose to call them the *nonexpressionist values of Beckett's aesthetic of reference*: language refers to, with nothing with which to refer, and nothing to which to refer. These negative values are as follows: 1. The *unplaceable*, questioning the right of building up spatial relations and of describing; 2. The *unpronominable*, which shakes the confidence in the power of nominating and predicating; 3. The *unrelatable*, which negates any ordering of Time.

In modern philosophies, the problems of Space and Time have been discussed within the antinomy of Realism and Idealism so that any attempt to expression implies the existence of a reality to be expressed. Expressionism is thus necessarily connected with realism. Should we say in reverse that nonexpressionism belongs to the idealist perspective? Considering the quasi-obsessive references Beckett made to certain forms of idealism, such as those of Descartes, Malebranche, Geulincx, Berkeley, Schopenhauer, one is tempted to agree. However, Beckett rejects idealism as well as realism for a very simple reason: he does not rely on philosophical reasoning, whatever it may be. It would be inappropriate to speak of the Beckettian idealism of Space and Time, or of his empirical or transcendental idealism of the Self. In consequence, I suggest we speak of a Beckettian *nonrealism* as different from idealism: to reject realism as basic structure for semantics and aesthetics is no reason to fall into the trap of idealism!

Critics have rarely analyzed the properties of the Beckettian space except indirectly and partially, from a narratological perspective. In this essay, I can but suggest a few aspects in Beckett's processes of *linguistic spatialization*. For him, the theory and praxis of space are not only related to its perception, but to its language and even more, in a matter of specific humor, to a special literary gift: "I who am so good at describing places, walls, ceilings, floors, they are my specialty, doors, windows, what haven't I imagined in the way of windows in the course of my career . . . nothing but the four surfaces, the six surfaces." A few pages later, in almost the same style he boasts: "I who am so good at topography." These gifts should be connected with another gift that Beckett claims more than once, the gift for logical constructions: logical order, spatial order have the same semiotic origin and belong to very similar functions in the poetic recreation of reality. Geometry and logic go together, but how?

Beckettian Space is not Euclidian-Kantian. It is not the classical tridimensional frame with the straight line and the right angle as basic forms, even if at times a Beckettian hero describes his disjointed walk as a rectilinear path through zigzags. It is not a Newtonian container within which objects are put in order and find their necessary coordinates. It is a *curved-and-hodological space*. It has a tendency to circularity, closeness, and closing. I borrow from Sartre's *Being and Nothingness* the concept of "hodological," which designates, as its etymology indicates, a space made of ways, roads, tracks, ditches, canals, which permits movements; it is a sort of spatial praxis, which has very little in common with the Promethean-Marxist praxis. It is also the place marked by impotence and failure. Its dynamics concerns, not progressive movements and accelerations, but repetitions, circularities, constant gyrations, seesaw motion, oscillations, coming and going, in brief, a turning and spiraling way that aspires to neutralizing linear, irreversible, and proversive movements, and desperately longs for a standstill. Here are a few typical quotations: "I had already advanced a good ten paces, if one may call them paces, not in a straight line I need hardly say, but in a sharp curve which, if I continued to follow it, seemed likely to restore me to my point of departure or to one adjacent. I must have got embroiled in a kind of inverted spiral, I mean one the coils of which, instead of widening more and more, grew narrower and narrower and finally, given the kind of space in which I was supposed to evolve, would come to an end for lack of room." "When I penetrate into that house, if I ever do, it will be to go on turning, faster and faster, more and more convulsive, like a constipated dog . . . until by virtue of a supreme spasm I am catapulted in the opposite direction and gradually leave backwards."

This curved space is also *globular*. "The space in which I was marooned being globular . . ." (in French: "L'espace où l'on m'avait foutu étant globulaire"). "I was under the impression I spent my life in spirals round the earth. Wrong, it's on the island I wind my endless ways. . . . When I come to the coast I turn back inland. And my course is not helicoidal, I got that wrong too, but a succession of irregular loops, now sharp and short as in the waltz, now of a parabolic sweep that embraces entire boglands, now between the two, somewhere or other, and invariably unpredictable in direction."

Hodological, curved, globular, the "unnamable" space is also more emptiness than fullness. More exactly, it is a bored-into space, a space made of holes. Beckett plays on the polysemy of "hole," meaning emptiness as well as open pit and abode, with a true need for it. "A hole in the earth, inhabited by Worm alone." Holes are connected with gaps: "Gaps, there have always been gaps"; in French: "Des trous, il y en a toujours eu." Furthermore, holes take on a special importance for the human body and its openings: "For if they could make a small hole for the eye, then bigger ones for the arms, they can make one bigger still for the transit of Worm, from darkness to light." Thus, the hole, as ultimate spatial expression in its ambivalence, is at the same time passage, place to hide and rest, unplaceability and void. This triple semantic perspective corresponds with the general linguistic situation. Actually, the objective, external space mirrors the characteristics of the universe of the words, which is prison, cage, vase, w.c., skull, etc. In brief, at these different levels, in the middle of objects or in the middle of words, the need for a place is a disguise for the need of void, the need for being and meaning a disguise for the appeal to nothingness and nonexpressiveness.

The experience of space-nothingness as a hole takes on another value which is present in the Beckettian opus from the beginning to the most recent: the concept of *space-partition*. "In this way they'll bring him to the wall" (in French: "Ils l'amèneront jusqu'à la cloison"), "and even to the precise point where they have made other holes through which to pass their arms and seize him." And let us read again this well-known text: "perhaps that's what I am, the thing that divides the world in two, on the one side the outside, on the other the inside, that can be as thin as foil, I'm neither one side nor the other, I'm in the middle, I'm the partition, I've two surfaces and no thickness, perhaps that is what I feel, myself vibrating, I'm the tympanum, on the one hand the mind, on the other the world, I don't belong to either." The hole leads to the spatial experience of rupture, separation; it is a place between places, a no-place between inside and outside. Space is finally a permanent fatality of division, a topographical impossibility.

Does such a situation refer to the Cartesian distinction between mind and space, soul and body? Yes, in a way, if we understand it as a distinction between inside and outside spaces, as a tension of simultaneous interior and exterior lives. However, Beckett never remains at this level of the individual experience of the spatial partition between soul and body. His Manichean cosmic sensibility transposes the problem of space into the problem of *light*. At the same time, in the same locus, our human reality is division and confusion of light and darkness. Pure division is felt as inaccessible limit. Confusion or "mess" is our lot. It possesses a double quality, physical and moral: grey and mess, as the categories of confusion show the same semantic connotation: "These lights gleaming low afar, then rearing up in a blaze and sweeping down upon me, blinding, to devour me." "But this question of light deserves to be treated in a section apart." "It's a nice grey, of the kind recommended as going with everything, urinous [in French: *pisseux*] and

warm." "Light is to close your eyes, that's where he must go, where it's
never dark, but here it's never dark either, it's they who make this grey,
with their lamps." "Enough now about holes. The grey means nothing, the
grey silence is not necessarily a mere lull, to be got through somehow, it
may be final, or it may not. But the lamps unattended will not burn on
forever, on the contrary they will go out, little by little, without attendants
to charge them anew, and go silent, in the end. Then it will be black. . . .
Worm will never know, let the silence be black or let it be grey, it can never
be known, as long as it lasts, whether it is final, or whether it is a mere
lull." "But this grey, this light, if he could escape from this light, which
makes him [Worm] suffer, is it not obvious it would make him suffer more
and more, in whatever direction he went, since he is at the center." "It's
he [the Devil] who showed me everything, here, in the dark, and how to
speak, and what to say, and a little nature, and a few names, and the outside
of men." Now let us quote from *Pour finir encore*, just to underscore the continuity of Beckett's *spatial aisthesis*: "Pour finir encore crâne seul dans le noir
lieu clos. . . . S'y lève enfin soudain ou peu `a peu et magique s'y maintient
un jour de plomb. Toujours un peu moins noir jusqu'au gris final . . . sable
gris à perte de vue sous un ciel même gris sans nuages." "Poussière grise
à perte de vue sous un ciel gris sans nuages et là soudain ou peu à peu où
poussière seule possible cette blancheur à déchiffrer." Space thus is dispersed
into a grey dust which recalls the "subtle matter" of Cartesian physics. Only
a voice remains in the dark: no object, no body is possible. And this is nothing
less than eddying words. Beckett leads us from the visual to the verbal space,
and the reverse, so that he checks any poetic attempt to a metaphorical sublimation à la Dante, from the physical hell to the spiritual and mystical heaven.
Such is the way he pursues his methodical dissociation of the language of
spatial references. His object-nonrealism becomes subject-nonrealism. By this
expression I mean that the disintegration of space into linguistic grey and
moral mess gives birth to the awareness of the impossibility of a subject,
of an I, be it empirical, transcendental, or metaphysical, as the responsible
source and warrant of writing. To complete its auto-destruction physics is
converted into psycholinguistics: the unplaceable refers the writer to the right
of nomination and grammatical subjectivity.

Such is the raison d'être of the passage from the first to the second
interrogation-exclamation "Who now?" suggesting a sort of fall from
"where" to "who." The problem of the subject is not lived and presented
by Beckett in a philosophical way, as it is with Descartes, Hume, or Kant.
Like space, where the problem of its essence and existence is identified with
the possibility or, more exactly, the impossibility of description, Beckett does

not try to find a theoretical answer to the question: What is the human self? He faces the problem that the writer has to solve: How can I create persons, characters, and, finally, how can I use the pronominal deictics of the first and second persons? In traditional literary criticism, this is known as the problem of characterization, i.e., the right, for the author and his/her creations, to say "I" and "you." In *Un* Beckett, testing the spatial language, is also testing the psychological language, insofar as it has to be centered around persons. This is why *Un* appears to be an *extreme attempt to create human beings with words*, and it is the definite recognition of the failure of doing so. In the first passages of the book, the author discards his former creations: "To tell the truth I believe they are all here, at least from Murphy on, I believe we are all here, but so far I have only seen Malone." And a few pages later: "All these Murphys, Molloys and Malones do not fool me. They have made me waste my time, suffer for nothing, speak of them when, in order to stop speaking, I should have spoken of me and of me alone." Earlier Beckett had already declared: "Method or no method, I shall have to banish them in the end, the beings, things, shapes, sounds and lights with which my haste to speak has encumbered this place." Such is the difference between *Un* and the preceding novels which accepted the principle of characterization, i.e., the right to choose surrogates, spokesmen. With *Un* the effort in creating the "pseudo-couple" Mahood-Worm is directly conscious of the relation between the two characters and the scriptor.

There, we witness a methodical destruction of subjectivity. One after the other the traditional techniques called for in the constitution of selves, with the help of proper names and pronouns, fail. First, the *incorporation* of the self in the case of Mahood. It is clear that the name Mahood suggests that Beckett tried to create a person with a human nature (the essence of manhood). Mahood is unable to achieve this project. The author is condemned to produce a monster, an incomplete space in body form: the subject cannot get its *corps propre* (body proper), as phenomenologists would say, i.e., its personal incorporation. Physical deformations which are present from the beginning of Beckett's writings reach their final state in *Un*. Mahood is reduced to a trunk without limbs, an eye which does not see, and a mouth full of words which do not belong to it. The body is just "the old vase in which I shall have accomplished my vicissitudes." Mahood has to be eliminated, not because he is a monster, but because he cannot give to the author-narrator a *subjective substance*. "I left it yesterday, Mahood's world, the street, the chophouse, the slaughter, the statue, and, through the railings, the sky like a slate-pencil. . . . The stories of Mahood are ended. He has realized they could not be about me, he has given up." Thus, there is no chance for a subject incarnating human nature, physically and mentally. There remains only one unique possibility: to go beyond species, biological or cultural.

Then, the scriptor, who still reserves the right to say "I" (in *Company* this right will be questioned), almost completely gives up the structures, however distorted and shaky they may be, of visual space. He concentrates on *audio-space*, this form being reduced to a nonlocalizable place where sounds from an unknown origin are perceived. The only reality is made of *voices*. "The fact is all this business about voices requires to be revised, corrected and then abandoned. Hearing nothing I am none the less a prey to communications. And I speak of voices! After all, why not, so long as one knows it's untrue." Everything becomes "a question of voices." Such is the appearance of Worm. "Now I seem to hear them say it is Worm's voice beginning, I pass on the news, for what it is worth." And this definitive remark: "Worm, be Worm, you'll see, it's impossible. . . . But it is solely a question of voices, no other image is appropriate." From here we are obsessively led to the opening sentence of *Company*: "A voice comes to one in the dark."

Voices are words, words are voices; space reaches its limits of *desincarnation, décorporation*, and referential doubt. It is no longer a world of things, but a world of words. More precisely, the world of things was already made of words, but ignored it. Within words, the scriptor (will he deserve the name of author?) finds the same characteristics as those of visual space: dominance of curves, and closeness, constant presence of holes, movement toward emptiness, seesaw between light and darkness, a permanent confusion and semantic mess against which he wages a losing fight. At least, it should be his duty, his fatality. One understands now why the principle of characterization reveals itself as impractical and artificial, source of psychological or sociological illusion. Subjectivity and its interior, classic or romantic universe are dissolved into a mist of words and meanings.

Below is a collage of quotations from *Un* that will illustrate the *fatal referential transfer from space to language*, from things to meanings: Spatial *desincarnation* is completed by the awareness that, if things are words, *the reverse is not true*. The linguistic universe subtends spatial structures and weakens them; then, the need for a place among things is changed into the place of a meaning among meanings; and that is the need of being a subject: Beckett explores Benveniste's principle of linguistic subjectivity, and finally destroys it:

"I'll say what I am . . . I'll fix their jargon for them . . . First I'll say what I'm not, that's how they taught me to proceed, then what I am." "Two holes and me in the middle, slightly choked. Or a single one, entrance and exit, where the words swarm and jostle like ants, hasty, indifferent, bringing nothing, taking nothing away, too light to leave a mark." "I'm in words, made of words, others' words, what others, the place too, the air, the walls, the ceiling, all words, the whole world is here with me, I'm the air, the walls, the walled-in one, everything yields, opens, ebbs, flows, like flakes, I'm all these flakes . . . I'm all these words, all these strangers, this dust of words." "Like a caged beast born of caged beasts."

The relation between subject and words cannot be settled by the characters and their proper names. Mahood is no help in assuring subjectivity and through it, referentiality. Worm also is a proper name without possible qualifications; he is deeper than the Unconscious, Freudian, or Jungian! He is an unname naming unnamability and silence. Then, in a parallel ordeal, Beckett tries the pronominal power, i.e., the personal deictics as a possible solution for the temporal "now" and the spatial "here." In *Un* the pronominal problematic is brought back to the basic tension between *I* and *they*, the right to say *I* as opposed to *they*, the singular first person against the plural and collective third person. In the modern philosophical tradition, the Cartesian cogito, followed by the Kantian transcendental Ego, maintained order between the *they*, putting them around the *I* who was like the Sun at the center of the Copernican system. But that idealistic solution, which very early obsessed the poet of "Whoroscope," is mystifying: Is it not the greatest lesson of modern sociology? Collective consciousness, i.e., the *they*, teaches me how, where and when to say *I*. My own language could be the product of a mystified *I* and of mystifying *they*. The human linguistic condition is a sort of Manichean semantic mess, with the absolute impossibility of separating meanings from each other. *Un* ends with this agnostic recognition: I do not know where I am, but I will continue to say *I* and to place myself in front of all the *they*. Such is the *pronominal tragedy* of language, as the final expression of semantic dispersion and confusion. Doubt about the placeable reveals itself as doubt about the pronominal, which is the ultimate decision for nomination and the last hope for an assured reference—*my* reference to *myself*. The well-known last statement of *Un*, "I can't go on, I'll go on" is more than the linguistic fatality of having to go on within language and its codes; it is *the fatality of saying I without knowing what it means*. At certain moments, the scriptor of *Un* wonders if the right pronoun would not be the impersonal deictic *that* (in French: *ça*) or *one* (in French: *on*). Without explaining why, Beckett does not explore this possibility. Maybe the answer should be sought thirty years later in the admirable poem entitled *Company*. Here the pronominal tragedy is relived, and the answer is—as the text proves by its almost total absence of *I*—a strict limitation of the discourse to the pronouns of second and third persons. "For the first personal and a fortiori plural pronoun had never any place in your vocabulary." The following text is a direct consequence of *Un* and its "ephectic" aporia: "Since he cannot think he will give up trying. Is there anything to add to this esquisse? H is *Unnamability*. Even M must go. So W reminds himself of his creature as so far created. W? But W too is creature. Figment."

Let us complete this analysis with a collage of *Un*'s comments on pronouns:

> But enough of this cursed first person [in French: "Cette putain de première personne"], it is really too red a herring, I'll get out of my depth if I am not careful. But, what then is the subject? Mahood? No, not yet. Worm? Even less. Bah, any old pronoun will do, provided one sees through it. . . . I shall not say I again, ever again, it's too farcical. I shall put in its place, whenever I hear it, the third person, if I think of it. . . . In the meantime no sense in bickering about pronouns and other parts of blather. The subject doesn't matter, there is none. Worm being in the singular, as it turned out, they are in the plural, to avoid confusion, confusion is better avoided, pending the great confounding . . . [notice the Manichean implications]. [Words] say they, speaking of them, to make me think it is I who am speaking. Or I say they, speaking of God knows what, to make me think it is not I who am speaking. . . . He wants me to be he . . . then he says I, as if I were he, or in another, let us be just. . . . He feels me in him, then he says I, as if I were he, or in another let us be just, then he says Murphy, or Molloy, I forget, as if I were Malone. . . . It's the fault of the pronouns, there is no name for me, no pronoun for me, all the trouble comes from that, that, it's a kind of pronoun too, it isn't that either, I'm not that either.

Space is inconsistent. Subject, whatever the pronoun, is illusory: geometry and grammar founder. All that remains for the prisoner-scriptor is one last way-out, one last interrogation: *Where now*? It concerns obviously the problem of Time, but not of the reality of Time. Time is only approachable through its *linguistic expression*, i.e., through narration. The need of story, Beckett recognizes it, is as strong as the need of description. But what can be done when space is dissolved and the subject unreferrable—two sorts of unnamability? Time itself is a superposition of discrete events, a heap which puzzled the Greek Sophists. In a very significant way, and following the Manichean denunciation of reality as confusion, Beckett rejects the clear-cut duality between time and eternity: the "now" of the three inaugurating questions is at the same time temporal and eternal; it is today surely, but also yesterday and tomorrow. Especially *I* does not refer to *hic et nunc*; another place, another time is always possible. Furthermore, because of the double impossibility of location and subjective enunciation, the third and ultimate impotence of language is experienced: the *unrelatable*. Far from announcing the era of the "new novel," Beckett, in his typical subdued manner, prophetizes the decline of the Narrative. It is evident that the relatable implies the assertive proposition, be it part of a description, of a story, or of a dialogue. However, to stop telling is not enough. Not enough either, to counterbalance patiently affirmations and negations, because that sort of balance dreamed of by the Sceptics does not break the syntactic structure of the proposition, and it continues to obey the principle of what logicians call "Truth-language."

That is why, in the first paragraph of *Un*, Beckett reviews the technique of Greek Scepticism: "How to proceed? By aporia pure and simple? Or by affirmations and negations invalidated as uttered, or sooner or later?" Then he confesses the real difficulty: "I say aporia without knowing what it means." He pursues: "Can one be ephectic otherwise than unawares?" After the interrogation left without an answer, he mentions the play with the "yesses and noes," and the paragraph ends in a state of pure confusion, simply overcome by the obligation to speak: "I shall never be silent. Never."

The question concerning the ephectics—those Sceptics who exercise by suspending their judgment—is central, and it gets a rhetorical, even grammatical, answer in the production of the text. Beckett finds out a technique of suspending one's judgment thanks to the *constant transfer of narrative assertion to the hypothesis or question-status*. That is why, from the first lines ("Unquestioning. I say, I. Unbelieving. Questions. Hypotheses, call them that") to the end of *Un*, the yesses and noes, counteracting their respective effects, *lose* their assertive power as well as their referential movement toward Truth or Reality, and they promote a paradoxical reference, which gives to *Un* its intense and tragic presence. The following quotes express this stylistic transference: "So they build up hypotheses that collapse on top of one another, it's human, a lobster couldn't do it." "Suppositions all equally vain, it's enough to enounce them to regret having spoken, familiar tourment." "Assume notably henceforward that the thing said and the thing heard have a common source, resisting for this purpose the temptation to call in question the possibility of assuming anything whatever." "Am I to suppose that I am inhabited, I can't suppose anything, I have to go on." "That's all hypotheses . . . it's a question of going on, it goes on, hypotheses are like everything else, they help you on, as if there were need of help." The same phrase "that's all hypotheses" is repeated and is connected with the act of naming: "I call that evening." Those remarks precede the extraordinary burlesque parody of a love story. Further on reappears "that's all hypotheses." Beckett then adds: "Lies, these gleams too, they were to save me, they were to devour me, that came to nothing."

We finally understand that the problems of space, subject, and time are one and the same, as simultaneous problems of description, subjectivation, and narration. They lead to the conversion and redirection of language into hypothetical zigzags. Because of their hypothetical nature, space, subject, and history cannot help the novelist in organizing his/her imaginary world and discourse. In consequence, the unnamable refers us to three basic limits: the unplaceable, the unpersonalizable, the unnarratable. Beckett tells us: Continue to use words at your own pleasure and fantasy, but do not pretend to build up with them harmonious worlds and histories for subjects and objects knowing what they are, where they stay, and when they come and go.

This is the secret meaning of the Beckettian phrase: "Imagination dead. Imagine." *Company* gives the conclusion, when *I* is replaced by a *one* who becomes a *you*. Such a narrative destruction begins with the following motif which plays the role of a musical and intellectual theme: "A voice comes to one in the dark, Imagine." And [. . .] the poet speaks of "the place to which imagination perhaps inadvisedly had consigned him." The last lines of *Company*, alloying pure poetry with pure criticism, are still answering the questions—the W-questions—of the *Unnamable*: "But with face upturned for good labour in vain at your fable. Till finally you hear how words are coming to an end. With every inane word a little nearer to the last. And how the fable too. The fable of one with you in the dark. The fable of one fabling of one with you in the dark. And how better in the end labour lost and silence. And you as you always were. Alone."

As a philosopher-reader and with the help of the Kantian theory of imagination, I propose to interpret Beckett's "fables" as *hypotheses of Imagination*, when Imagination realizes that it cannot achieve the idealist dream of reconstructing the world and the self in the same verbal effort, or it cannot apply to writing the vain principle of imitation which governs any sort of aesthetic realism. There is no literary virtue such as idealist or realist sincerity, or at least, these virtues belonged to a period of dogmatic narrative when the novelists ignored the dubious status of their ontological presuppositions. Now we should know that Space, Subjectivity, and Time are products of our linguistic imagination. They are but verbal hypotheses. As such, i.e., when they become aware of being imaginary forms, they can but undo themselves to escape from the ontological illusions occasioned by the natural, noncritical praxis of language. Beckett's works mark the successive phases of an infinite struggle within writing, not for Truth or Reality, but for its own and pure survival. Novels, plays, or poems stand between poetry and criticism: deeply sceptic of their means and ends, they play a cat-and-mouse game between spontaneity and reflection, between poetry and philosophy. Fundamentally, Beckett is a poet, and who else could be the sincere writer? He would like to "express" and to "refer," but in a nonexpressive, nonreferential way, rediscovering the pictorial and musical powers of words as meanings. He uses philosophical techniques for literary purposes, beyond the fallacious pretense of finding truth or creating reality. He borrowed from philosophy its most radical problematics, but rejected any attempt to systematizing discourses. It would be absurd to look for a Beckettian theory of Space, Time, or Consciousness. For the poet those three words polarize linguistic extensions and restrictions. The Beckettian corpus tells us the humorous Odysseus of successive essays—failures to go more and more beyond the spatial-temporal-subjective order which gave to Western texts their grammatical and rational organizations. Beckett's exercises in impotence witness the will of reaching a stage which is not the "ineffable," the obscure night and luminous silence of the mystics, but pure poetry, when reference makes sense, originary rhythm, language returning to its "fundamental sounds," grammar and semantics subjected to the pitiless sincerity of philology.

Such is the linguistic lesson of *The Unnamable*, when and where the writer explores the virtualities of language for our century: the writer can no more assume the rights revendicated by the romanesque dream, even when that dream becomes an exercise in deconstructing its structures. Anti-novels, new novels, continue to rely on the objectivity of Space, the subjectivity of characters, and the causality of Time. Thus the Beckettian triple interrogation has no answer. The awareness of it is the proper life of *Un*, a text without beginning and end, starting and closing again and again, the only valid introduction, not to the "general grammar" thanks to which Port-Royalists and Encyclopedists hoped to justify our modernity, that is to say, our will to linguistic power and intoxication, but to the primitive energy of language. Nothing is more real than nothing: this metaphysical principle that Beckett liked to quote in *Murphy*, hides an aesthetic credo: the act of poetic faith in language is the only condition for feeling oneself real; the rest is vain literature and artificial paradise!

Let us give the last word to the linguist and ask him/her what to say about the Beckettian exercise in nonexpressionism. In *Unspeakable Sentences*, at the end of a chapter entitled "Subjectivity and Sentences of Direct and Indirect Speech," Ann Banfield convincingly states: "Direct speech is at once expression and communication. On the other hand, thought, reported in the subordinate S of indirect speech, is always reduced to its content; it is not only not communication, it is also nonexpressive" (*Unspeakable Sentences: Narration and Representation in the Language of Fiction*). Linguists look for the characteristics of natural-normal language, especially when they follow the Chomskian belief in "universal grammar." To them *Un* may appear as a puzzling challenge. Here is the most direct speech one can imagine whose objectives are the destruction of communicative and expressive codes. Actually Beckett does not obfuscate communication or annihilate expressive powers; nor does he fall into the sophistic trap of communicating noncommunication, nor of being so expressive that he demystifies expressive powers. He simply uses direct speech as if it were—not indirect speech, but what German criticism calls *erlebte rede* and the French grammarians *discours indirect libre*. At the level of *Un*, Beckett's writing becomes "discours *direct* libre," i.e., language destructing bound variables and reducing grammatical deictics to anaphoric relations. Pronouns, as bound variables, are referred to an unnamable pronoun-source of all texts; spatial and temporal deictics (here and now) are subordinated to a "then" as the weakest possible liaison between linguistic systems and processes, so that ultimately the pitiless disorganization of the deictic codes produces an extraordinary effect of intense and conscious referentiality: in the linguistic field, nothing is more real and sincere than the unnamable in its own discourse, nothing is more communicative and expressive than the direct refusal to express and communicate; that is poetry for itself.

Chronology

1906	Born Good Friday, April 13, at Foxrock, near Dublin, second son of William and Mary Beckett, middle-class Irish Protestants.
1919–23	Attends Portora Royal School, Enniskillen, a traditional Anglo-Irish boarding school.
1923–27	Attends Trinity College, Dublin; Bachelor of Arts in French and Italian.
1928	Begins two-year fellowship at Ecole Normale Supérieure in Paris. Friendship with Joyce begins, as does immersion in the work of Descartes.
1929	Early writings in *Transition.*
1930	*Whoroscope* wins competition for best poem on the subject of time.
1931	*Proust* published. Returns to Dublin as assistant to Professor of Romance Languages at Trinity. *Le Kid,* parody of Corneille.
1932	Writes unpublished *Dream of Fair to Middling Women.*
1933	Death of William Beckett. Begins three-year stay in London.
1934	*More Pricks than Kicks.*
1936	Travels in Germany. *Echo's Bones.*
1937	Returns to Paris.
1938	Sustains serious stab wound from stranger. Begins relationship with Suzanne Dumesnil. *Murphy.*
1939	Returns to Paris after Irish sojourn.
1940	Is active in French Resistance movement.
1942	Flees to unoccupied France to escape Gestapo. Works as day laborer for two years in farming. Writes *Watt.*
1945	Goes to Ireland after German surrender. Returns to France for service with Irish Red Cross. Returns to Paris permanently.
1946–50	Productive period of writing in French, including the trilogy *Molloy, Malone meurt,* and *L'Innommable,* and the play *En attendant Godot.*

145

1947   *Murphy* published in French.
1950   Visits Ireland at the time of his mother's death.
1951   *Molloy* published. *Malone meurt* published.
1952   *Godot* published.
1953   First performance of *Godot* in Paris. *Watt* published. *L'Innom-mable* published.
1955   *Waiting for Godot* opens in London.
1956   *Waiting for Godot* opens in Miami, Florida, for first American performance.
1957   *All That Fall* broadcast by BBC. *Fin de partie* published; first performance (in French) in London.
1958   *Krapp's Last Tape* and *Endgame* (in English) open in London.
1959   *Embers* broadcast by BBC. Honorary degree from Trinity College, Dublin.
1961   *Comment c'est* published. *Happy Days* opens in New York City. Shares, with Borges, International Publishers' Prize.
1962   Marries Suzanne Dumesnil, March 25. *Words and Music* broadcast by BBC.
1963   *Play* performed at Ulm. *Cascando* broadcast in Paris.
1964   Goes to New York City to help produce his *Film* (with Buster Keaton).
1969   Nobel Prize in literature.
1972   *The Lost Ones.*
1973   *Not I.*
1976   *Ends and Odds; Fizzles; All Strange Away.*
1977   *. . . but the clouds . . .*
1978   *Mirlitonnades* (35 short poems).
1980   *Company; One Evening.*
1981   *Ill Seen Ill Said; Rockaby.* *Quad*, a mime play.
1983   *Catastrophe. Worstward Ho.*

Contributors

HAROLD BLOOM, Sterling Professor of the Humanities at Yale University, is the author of *The Anxiety of Influence*, *Poetry and Repression*, and many other volumes of literary criticism. His forthcoming study, *Freud: Transference and Authority*, attempts a full-scale reading of all of Freud's major writings. A MacArthur Prize Fellow, he is general editor of five series of literary criticism published by Chelsea House. During 1987–88, he served as Charles Eliot Norton Professor of Poetry at Harvard University.

GEORGES BATAILLE, who died in 1962, was a French poet, novelist, and philosopher. He founded, in 1946, the journal *Critique*, one of the most influential of the postwar period. He is the author of *Literature and Evil*, *The Story of the Eye*, *Lascaux: Or, the Birth of Art*, and *Death and Sensuality: A Study of Eroticism and the Taboo*.

MAURICE BLANCHOT has published hundreds of essays and some two dozen books. Those available in English range from novels and shorter fictions (*Thomas the Obscure*, *Death Sentence*, *The Madness of the Day*, and *Time Comes*) to works in literary criticism and theory, political theory and analysis, and philosophy (*The Sirens' Song*, *The Space of Literature*, *The Writing of the Disaster*, and *The Gaze of Orpheus*).

HUGH KENNER, Professor Emeritus of English at The Johns Hopkins University, is the leading critic of the High Modernists (Pound, Eliot, Joyce) and of Beckett. His books include *The Pound Era*, *The Stoic Comedians*, *Dublin's Joyce*, and *Ulysses*.

LEO BERSANI is Chairman of the Department of French at the University of California, Berkeley. He is the author of several books including *Marcel Proust: The Fictions of Life and Art*, *Balzac to Beckett: Center and Circumference in French Fiction*, *A Future for Astyanax: Character and Desire in Literature*, *Freud and Baudelaire*, and *The Death of Stéphane Mallarmé*.

WOLFGANG ISER teaches English and Comparative Literature at the Universität Konstanz in Germany and the University of California, Irvine. A pioneer of "reception aesthetics" criticism and a founder of the "Poetics and Hermeneutics" research group, he has written books on Fielding, Pater, Spenser, and Beckett as well as *The Act of Reading*, *The Implied Reader*, and *Der Appelstruktur der Texte*.

LESLIE HILL is Lecturer in the Department of French at the University of Warwick, England. He has written extensively on Beckett, as well as on the nouveau roman.

CHARLOTTE RENNER teaches in the Department of English at the Portland School of Art, in Portland, Maine.

ROCH C. SMITH is Professor of French and Spanish at the University of North Carolina, Greensboro. He is the author of books on André Malraux and Gaston Bachelard.

H. PORTER ABBOTT is Professor of English at the University of California, Santa Barbara. He is the author of *The Fiction of Samuel Beckett: Form and Effect* and *Diary Fiction: Writing as Action*.

EDOUARD MOROT-SIR is W. R. Kenan, Jr., Professor Emeritus at the University of North Carolina at Chapel Hill. He has served as French Cultural Attaché to the United States. His books include *La Pensée negative*, *La Pensée française aujourd'hui*, and *La Métaphysique de Pascal*.

Bibliography

Abbott, H. Porter. *The Fiction of Samuel Beckett: Form and Effect.* Berkeley: University of California Press, 1973.

Acheson, James. "The Art of Failure: Samuel Beckett's *Molloy.*" *Southern Humanities Review* 17 (1983): 1–18.

Bair, Deirdre. *Samuel Beckett.* New York: Harcourt, Brace, Jovanovich, 1978.

Baldwin, Helen Louise. *Samuel Beckett's Real Silence.* University Park: Pennsylvania State University Press, 1981.

Beja, Morris, S. E. Gontarski, and Pierre Astier, eds. *Samuel Beckett: Humanistic Perspectives.* Columbus: Ohio State University Press, 1983.

Berengo, Adriano. "Samuel Beckett: 'The Mania for Symmetry.' " *Gradiva* 1 (1976): 21–37.

Bernal, Olga. *Langage et fiction dans le roman de Beckett.* Paris: Gallimard, 1969.

Bloom, Harold, ed. *Modern Critical Views: Samuel Beckett*, New Haven: Chelsea House, 1986.

Boulais, Véronique. "Samuel Beckett: une écriture en mal de je." *Poétique* 17 (1974): 114–32.

Bové, Paul. "Beckett's Dreadful Postmodern: The Deconstruction of Form in *Molloy.*" In *De-structing the Novel: Essays in Applied Postmodern Hermeneutics*, edited by Leonard Orr, 185–221. Troy, N.Y.: Whitston, 1982.

Chambers, Ross. "Beckett's Brinkmanship." *AUMLA* 19 (May 1963): 57–75.

Christensen, Inger. *The Meaning of Metafiction.* Bergen, Oslo, Troms: Universitetsforlaget, 1981.

Coe, Richard N. *Samuel Beckett.* New York: Grove, 1970.

Cohn, Ruby. *Back to Beckett.* Princeton: Princeton University Press, 1973.

———. *Samuel Beckett, The Comic Gamut.* New Brunswick, N.J.: Rutgers University Press, 1962.

———, ed. *Samuel Beckett: A Collection of Criticism.* New York: McGraw-Hill, 1975.

Copeland, Hannah Case. *Art and the Artist in the Works of Samuel Beckett.* The Hague: Mouton, 1975.

Dearlove, J. E. *Accommodating the Chaos: Samuel Beckett's Nonrelational Art.* Durham, N.C.: Duke University Press, 1982.

Doherty, Francis. *Samuel Beckett.* London: Hutchinson University Library, 1971.

Esslin, Martin. *Samuel Beckett, A Collection of Critical Essays.* Englewood Cliffs, N. J.: Prentice-Hall, 1965.

Federman, Raymond. *Journey to Chaos, Samuel Beckett's Early Fiction*. Berkeley: University of California Press, 1965.

Federman, Raymond, and Lawrence Graver, eds. *Samuel Beckett, the Critical Heritage*. Boston: Routledge & Kegan Paul, 1979.

Fitch, Brian. "*L'innommable* and the Hermeneutic Paradigm." *Chicago Review* 33 (1982): 100–106.

Fletcher, John. *The Novels of Samuel Beckett*. London: Chatto & Windus, 1964.

———. *Samuel Beckett's Art*. London: Chatto & Windus, 1967.

Friedman, Alan W., Charles Rossman, and Dina Herzer, eds. *Beckett Translating/Translating Beckett*. University Park: Pennsylvania State University Press, 1986.

Friedman, Melvin J., ed. *Samuel Beckett Now, Critical Approaches to His Novels*. Chicago: University of Chicago Press, 1970.

Garis, Robert. "Journalist and Critic." *Hudson Review* 19 (1966): 178–86.

Gontarski, S. E., ed. *On Beckett: Essays and Criticism*. New York: Grove, 1986.

Gurewitch, Morton. "Beckett and the Comedy of Decomposition." *Chicago Review* 33 (1982): 93–99.

Hassan, Ihab Habib. *The Literature of Silence, Henry Miller and Samuel Beckett*. New York: Knopf, 1967.

Hayman, Ronald. *Samuel Beckett*. New York: Ungar, 1973.

Hesla, David H. *The Shape of Chaos, An Interpretation of the Art of Samuel Beckett*. Minneapolis: University of Minnesota Press, 1971.

Hill, Leslie. "The Name, the Body, *The Unnamable*." *The Oxford Literary Review* 6 (1983): 52–67.

Hoffman, Frederick John. *Samuel Beckett: The Language of Self*. Carbondale: Southern Illinois University Press, 1962.

Iser, Wolfgang. "When is the end not the end? The idea of fiction in Beckett." In *The Implied Reader: Patterns of Communication in Prose Fiction from Bunyan to Beckett*, 257–73. Baltimore and London: The Johns Hopkins University Press, 1974.

Kellman, Steven. *The Self-Begetting Novel*. New York: Columbia University Press, 1980.

Kenner, Hugh. *Flaubert, Joyce and Beckett: The Stoic Comedians*. Boston: Beacon Press, 1962.

———. *Samuel Beckett: A Critical Study*. New York: Grove, 1961. New edition with a supplementary chapter. Berkeley: University of California Press, 1968.

———. *A Reader's Guide to Samuel Beckett*. New York: Farrar, Straus & Giroux, 1973.

Lee, Robin. "The Fictional Topography of Samuel Beckett." In *The Modern English Novel: The reader, the writer and the work*, edited by Gabriel Josipovici, 206–24. New York: Harper & Row, 1976.

Lyons, Charles R. *Samuel Beckett*. London: Macmillan, 1983.

Macksey, Richard. "The Artist in the Labyrinth: Design or *Dasein*." *MLN* 77 (1962): 239–56.

Modern Fiction Studies 29 (Spring 1983). Special Samuel Beckett issue.

Moorjani, Angela. *Abysmal Games in the Novels of Samuel Beckett*. Chapel Hill: University of North Carolina Press, 1982.

Morot-Sir, Edouard, H. Harper and D. McMillan, eds. *Samuel Beckett: The Art of Rhetoric*. Chapel Hill: University of North Carolina Press, 1976.

O'Hara, J. D. *Twentieth-Century Interpretations of* Molloy, Malone Dies, The Unnamable. Englewood Cliffs, N. J.: Prentice Hall, 1970.

Pilling, John. *Samuel Beckett*. Boston: Routledge & Kegan Paul, 1976.

Rabinovitz, Rubin. *The Development of Samuel Beckett's Fiction*. Urbana: University of Illinois Press, 1984.

Robinson, Michael. *The Long Sonata of the Dead: A Study of Samuel Beckett*. New York: Grove, 1970.

Rosen, Steven J. *Samuel Beckett and the Pessimistic Tradition*. New Brunswick, N. J.: Rutgers University Press, 1976.

Saint-Martin, Fernande. *Samuel Beckett et l'univers de la fiction*. Montreal: University of Montreal Press, 1976.

Scherzer, Dina. *Structure de la trilogie de Beckett:* Molloy, Malone meurt, L'Innommable. The Hague: Mouton, 1976.

Schulz, Hans-Joachim. *This Hell of Stories: A Hegelian Approach to the Novels of Samuel Beckett*. The Hague: Mouton, 1973.

Scott, Nathan Alexander. *Samuel Beckett*. New York: Hillary House, 1969.

Solomon, Philip. *The Life after Birth: Imagery in Samuel Beckett's Trilogy*. University: Mississippi University Romance Monographs, 1975.

Webb, Eugene. *Samuel Beckett: A Study of His Novels*. Seattle: University of Washington Press, 1970.

Acknowledgments

"Molloy's Silence" by Georges Bataille from *Samuel Beckett: The Critical Heritage,* edited by Lawrence Graves and Raymond Federman, © 1979 by Lawrence Graves and Raymond Federman. Reprinted by permission of Routledge & Kegan Paul Ltd.

"Where Now? Who Now?" by Maurice Blanchot from *The Sirens' Song,* edited by Gabriel Josipovici, © 1982 by the Harvester Press Ltd. Reprinted by permission of the Harvester Press Ltd. and Indiana University Press.

"The Trilogy" by Hugh Kenner from *A Reader's Guide to Samuel Beckett* by Hugh Kenner, © 1973 by Thames & Hudson Ltd. Reprinted by permission of Thames & Hudson Ltd.

"Beckett and the End of Literature" (originally entitled "Beckett and the End of Literature [The Trilogy: *Molloy, Malone Meurt,* and *L'Innommable*]") by Leo Bersani from *Balzac to Beckett: Center and Circumference in French Fiction* by Leo Bersani, © 1970 by Leo Bersani. Reprinted by permission.

"Subjectivity as the Autogenous Cancellation of Its Own Manifestations" (originally entitled "Subjectivity as the Autogenous Cancellation of Its Own Manifestations: Samuel Beckett: *Molloy, Malone Dies, The Unnamable*") by Wolfgang Iser from *The Implied Reader: Patterns of Communication in Prose Fiction from Bunyan to Beckett* by Wolfgang Iser, © 1974 by The Johns Hopkins University Press, Baltimore/London. Reprinted by permission of the Johns Hopkins University Press.

"Fiction, Myth, and Identity in Samuel Beckett's Novel Trilogy" by Leslie Hill from *Forum for Modern Language Studies* 13, no. 3 (July 1977), © 1977 by Leslie Hill. Reprinted by permission of the author and *Forum for Modern Language Studies.*

"The Self-Multiplying Narrators of *Molloy, Malone Dies,* and *The Unnamable*" by Charlotte Renner from *The Journal of Narrative Technique* 11, no. 1 (Winter 1981), © 1981 by *The Journal of Narrative Technique.* Reprinted by permission.

"Naming the M/inotaur: Beckett's Trilogy and the Failure of Narrative" by Roch C. Smith from *Modern Fiction Studies* 29, no. 1 (Spring 1983), © 1983 by Purdue Research Foundation. Reprinted by permission of the Purdue Research Foundation, West Lafayette, Indiana.

"The Harpooned Notebook: *Malone Dies*" (originally entitled "The Harpooned Notebook: *Malone Dies* and Conventions of Intercalated Narrative") by H. Porter Abbott from *Samuel Beckett: Humanistic Perspectives,* edited by Morris Beja, S. E. Gonatarski and Pierre Astier, © 1983 by the Ohio State University Press. Reprinted by permission.

"Grammatical Identity in *The Unnamable*" (originally entitled "Grammatical Identity and Samuel Beckett's Non-Expressionism: Space, Subjectivity, and Time in *The Unnamable*") by Edouard Morot-Sir from *Writing in a Modern Temper: Essays on French Literature and Thought in Honor of Henri Peyre* (Stanford French and Italian Studies 3), edited by Mary Ann Caws, © 1984 by ANMA Libri & Co. Reprinted by permission of ANMA Libri & Co.

Index